A CRITICAL THEORY OF LITERATURE

A Critical Theory of Literature

Costanzo Di Girolamo

THE UNIVERSITY OF WISCONSIN PRESS

Published in English 1981

The University of Wisconsin Press
114 North Murray Street
Madison, Wisconsin 53715

The University of Wisconsin Press, Ltd.
1 Gower Street
London WC1E 6HA, England

First printing in English

Printed in the United States of America

For LC CIP information see the colophon

ISBN 0–299–08120–6

Contents

Preface

A few preliminary words will be necessary to justify the limits and aims of this book.

I should first of all point out that the survey of literary theories outlined here is partial and instrumental. It was not my intention to write a history, not even a critical history, of twentieth-century views on literature. The reader may find a more complete picture in existent works, of a size and purpose far different from this. I have instead concentrated on those aspects which seem to be the most significant and symptomatic of modern thought on literary language, its functions and its properties, paying special attention to the antonomastic exponents of the leading methodologies.

As far as the rhetorical strategy of the book is concerned, from the outset I gave up any attempt at creating suspense. The central theses are already implicit in the introductory chapter, which is the only section of the book calling for a minimum effort in following a number of linguistic concepts that, however, are never taken for granted.

This work is not intended to address an audience composed exclusively of semioticians; rather, it attempts to approach from an interdisciplinary standpoint a whole series of problems which every consumer of literature, professional or not, may come across. I feel therefore that I should apologize to erudite readers for some stylistic fluctuations, and for having tended to make this study more of an essay than a piece of academic investigation. But it will soon become clear that my purpose is not so much to build a new, organic theory of literature as to provide the bases for a critique of the very concept of the literary. I do not deny the possibility of nor the need for a constructive intervention to follow a destructive action: basically, Chapters 6–10 will suggest, at least hypothetically, possible solutions to the problems posed in Chapters 1–5. However, very few operative instructions may be provided here and now for laying new foundations for a discipline whose very presuppositions must instead be reconsidered.

With this program in mind, I believed it possible to privilege one point of view—that of Hjelmslev's glossematics—which is presented and discussed, insofar as it concerns our inquiry, in the Introduction. The theory of language proposed by Hjelmslev in a book that remains a classic of twentieth-century linguistics has already been applied to poetics. The way it is used here, however, differs radically from previous applications, since I believe that its relevance to literary studies is much less obvious than others have thought, and that it touches only indirectly upon the problem of literature. Nevertheless, in Hjelmslev's original project, glossematics should have shifted from the level of a linguistic theory to that of a general theory of communication, once the procedure elaborated for the description of natural language had been expanded to cover every kind of semiotic system, until it again grasped the communicative process in all its complexity. Although this program remained incomplete for the most part, the theoretical model proposed by Hjelmslev seems to me full of suggestions for an integrated consideration of the various aspects of the literary fact, as well as a valid critical tool to be used against partial and dogmatic approaches that still dominate literary theory.

Obviously, a different way of conceiving the problems of literature, and more generally of art and artistic production, may only be perceived in the distance. This book neither aims nor could aim at being anything more than the beginning of a discussion, to be continued and refined: a motion, therefore, to debate, or better still, to put everything into question.

Baltimore, September 1978

A CRITICAL THEORY OF LITERATURE

Introduction:
Glossematics and the Theory
of Literature

The closing pages of Hjelmslev's *Prolegomena to a Theory of Language*, since their first edition in Danish (1943), have often inspired applications in the theory of literature. In particular, Chapter 22, "Connotative Semiotics and Metasemiotics," seemed rich in suggestions, though not in explicit directions, for the use of the glossematic model in literary analysis. And Hjelmslev himself repeatedly states that linguistic theory, in its fullest stage of development, should include the study of the literary fact among its aims. Nevertheless, the enthusiasm shown for these few pages by an entire generation of semiotically oriented critics and poeticians does not seem to correspond to an adequate understanding of their meaning and of their immediate or indirect implications. The purpose of the present discussion, which is to be the starting point of our inquiry, is not so much to carry out an exercise in glossematic philology as to shed some light on one of the most problematic passages in the *Prolegomena*, and to provide the bases for a more profitable and less instrumental application of Hjelmslev's hypotheses to the theory of the literary text.

For Hjelmslev, as for Saussure before him, language is a system of signs, a semiotic, analogous to other semiotics. In it may be identified, therefore, an expression plane (E) and a content plane (C), between which there is a relationship, called sign function:

$$\frac{E}{C}$$

This model, a denotative semiotic in Hjelmslev's terms, is nevertheless insufficient to represent the complexity of even the simplest of communicative acts, into which more than one semiotic system comes into play. "In order to establish a simple model situation we have worked with the premiss that the given text displays structural homogeneity, that we are justified in encatalyzing one and only one semiotic system to a text. This premiss, however, does not hold good in practice. On the contrary, any text that is not of so small extension that it fails to yield a sufficient basis for deducing a system generalizable to other texts usually contains derivates that rest on different systems" [115]. A list then follows of what will be defined on the next page as connotators—stylistic forms, styles, value-styles, media (speech, writing, gesture, flag code, etc.), tones, idioms (vernaculars, national languages, regional languages, physiognomies)—but Hjelmslev does not claim that this list is exhaustive.

In textual analysis connotators appear "as parts that enter into functives in such a way that the functives have mutual substitution when these parts are deducted" [118]. The deduction of the connotators from the functives involved allows for the mutual substitution of the functives, thus making the functives bound variants or varieties. For instance, if x and y are signs differing only in that each is solidary with its own connotator (x with K_1 and y with K_2), then, once K_1 is deducted from x and K_2 from y, x and y are correlated by mutual substitution. An elementary example may be provided by the lexicon. Many terms may be substituted for each other—that is, they are "synonyms"—if the connotators distinguishing them are removed. Words (functives) like *girl*, *maiden*, *lassie*, and *gal* are synonymous (bound variants or varieties) once the connotators with which they are solidary have been deducted: "learned" for *maiden*, "Scottish" for *lassie*, and "slang" for *gal*, while *girl* is an unmarked term, used in "standard" English, which is thus its connotator. A similar discourse could also apply to phenomena of pronunciation, morphology, syntax, and so on.

On the other hand the connotators themselves are objects "whose treatment belongs to semiotics. Their treatment . . . belongs to a special discipline which determines the study of denotative semiotics" [118]. The solidarity existing between certain sign classes and certain connotators is a sign function, "since the sign classes are *expression* for the connotators as *content*" [118]. From this derives the definition of a connotative semiotic: "Thus it seems appropriate to view the connotators as content for which the denotative semiotics are expression, and to designate this content and this expression as a *semiotic*, namely a *connotative semiotic*. . . . Thus a connotative semiotic is a semiotic that is not a language, and one whose expression plane is provided by the content plane and expression plane of a denotative semiotic. Thus it is a semiotic one plane of which (namely the expression plane) is a semiotic" [119]. Graphically:

$$\begin{array}{c} \underline{\qquad E \qquad} \\ \underline{\qquad C \qquad} \\ C \end{array}$$

As opposed to the connotative semiotic, a metasemiotic, coinciding with linguistics, is a semiotic whose content plane is provided by a denotative semiotic:

$$\begin{array}{c} \underline{\qquad E \qquad} \\ \underline{\qquad E \qquad} \\ C \end{array}$$

Finally, Hjelmslev postulates a metasemiotic of the connotative semiotic, whose content plane is a connotative semiotic:

$$\begin{array}{c} \underline{\qquad E \qquad} \\ \underline{\qquad E \qquad} \\ \underline{\qquad C \qquad} \\ C \end{array}$$

and a metasemiology, whose content plane is a metasemiotic, or a semiology:

$$
\begin{array}{c}
\underline{\text{E}} \\
\underline{\text{E}} \\
\underline{\text{E}} \\
\text{C}
\end{array}
$$

Nevertheless, while Hjelmslev explicitly names the metasemiotic "a semiotic that treats of a semiotic; . . . such a metasemiotic linguistics itself must be" [119–20], he does not clearly indicate the nature of the connotative semiotic. Yet it is here, at the point of definition of the connotative semiotic, that many readers have readily identified it with literature. Thus it is a short step to the formulation of the following equations: standard language = denotative semiotic, literary language = connotative semiotic.

A short history of this interpretation must begin with Roland Barthes, who was the first to divulge (and distort) Hjelmslev's notion of connotative semiotic, in his *Eléments de sémiologie*. Apart from mistakenly attributing the connotators to the expression plane of a connotative semiotic [1964: 91], while for Hjelmslev these make up the content plane [1943: 118], Barthes writes: "We shall therefore say that a *connoted system is a system whose expression plane is itself constituted by a signifying system*: the common cases of connotation will of course consist of complex systems of which language forms the first system (this is, for instance, the case with literature)" [1964: 89]. Many others have followed in Barthes's footsteps: Marie-Noëlle Gary-Prieur, "Literature fits the definition of connotative language, because it is a system whose expression plane is provided by language (denotative language)" [1971: 105]; Cesare Segre, "The semiotic of a literary language is connotative with respect to the semiotic of common language which is denotative" [1969: 49]; etc. Likewise, Bertha Siertsema opposes the connotative semiotics to "an ordinary (I might say 'uncoloured') language (i.e. a 'denotative semiotic')" [1955: 213]; while Paul Zumthor observes that the definition of literature as a message concentrated upon itself "resembles that which Hjelmslev gives for semiotic connotive systems" [1975: 203]. More serious still is the misunderstanding of some linguists, who have gone so far as freely to distort the letter, the terminology, and the very meaning of the original. According to the text grammarian van Dijk, "even important linguists like Hjelmslev have attempted to characterize poetic language, that is, poetic style, by formally distinguishing between *connotative* and *denotative*, so that connotative languages would have the content and expression planes of a denotative language as their expression plane, thus giving rise to a specific 'connotative content,' that may be identified with the aesthetic or literary 'meaning' of the texts, in which such operations appear" [1972*a*: 155].

In the *Prolegomena*, Hjelmslev does indeed mention literature several times and insists on the need for establishing the "literary science" [102] on a new foundation; but oddly enough, the allusions to literature in these pages are rather indirect. Only a vague reference is made when he distinguishes "different *stylistic forms* (character-ized by various restrictions: verse, prose, various blends of the two)" as types of connotators [115]. In fact, a closer and less biased read-ing of the passage in question excludes the possibility of Hjelmslev's referring to literature here, or rather of his referring to literature in particular. On the contrary, we have seen that the connotators, as "derivates that rest on a different system" [115], cannot be deleted from any text. Every text, for example, must necessarily have as a connotator the idiom in which it is written: "English" for the *Can-terbury Tales*, "Danish" for the original edition of the *Prolegomena*, and so on, as well as the inevitable connotators of stylistic form, media (speech or writing), and the like. In this sense there is no text which is without connotators and which cannot be viewed as a con-notative semiotic. So we might add that there exists a connotative semiotic of a metasemiotic too; no one could prevent me, for in-stance, from carrying out a stylistic analysis of Hjelmslev's prose:

$$
\begin{array}{|c|}
\hline
E \\
\hline
E \\
\hline
C \\
\hline
C \\
\hline
\end{array}
$$

although in deference to the simplicity principle [18] this figure may be interpreted as a connotative semiotic, whose expression plane is a denotative semiotic with a biplanar content.

Consequently, a purely denotative semiotic not only cannot be identified with standard language, but it has no other existence except as a temporary moment in the analysis. "In its point of departure," Hjelmslev says, "linguistic theory was established as immanent, with constancy, system, and internal function as its sole aims, to the apparent cost of fluctuation and nuance, life and concrete physical and phenomenological reality. A temporary restriction of the field of vision was the price that had to be paid to elicit from language itself its secret. But precisely through that immanent point of view and by virtue of it, language itself returns the price that it demanded" [127]. In fact, "the smallest system is a self-sufficient totality, but no totality is isolated" [126].

The distinction between denotative semiotics on the one hand, and connotative semiotics and metasemiotics on the other, should not be considered a recognition of different "types" of language (standard language, literary language, and metalanguage), but depends entirely on the viewpoint of the analysis, while the object, as well as the method, of analysis remains the same.

Equally unfounded, at least with respect to its theoretical premises, is another reformulation or interpretation of this point in Hjelmslev's theory which actually originated in the glossematic milieu itself. According to Stender-Petersen, connotation consists of the "instrumentalization occurring . . . in the expression plane of the literary art," which "is accompanied in the content plane by a phenomenon that I should be tempted to consider as a chain of emotions, not of notions of emotions, but precisely as a chain of the emotions themselves" [1949: 282]. In a similar vein, Johansen conceives the connotators as a complex of mental associations, symbols, and metaphoric usages; for instance, "the general connotation of *lion*" would be "something powerfully vital, evoking a sense of the force of nature, especially of a fierce, though noble and majestic force" [1949: 296–97]. For Segre too, "'denotation' is the significative nucleus of a word, that which, to make it clear, is found in dictionary definitions. Instead, 'connotation' is, so to speak, the aura of suggestions surrounding the word, through associations of ideas, environmental references, phonic effects, and so on. Obviously the writer's action more often plays on 'connotation' than on 'denotation:' if he were to ill-treat the latter too much, he would risk not being understood. At most the writer may sometimes try to make a new or unusual 'denotation' comprehensible by playing on the 'connotation'" [1970: 334]. Thus the traditional conception of connotation (as found, for example, in Bloomfield [1933: 151–54]) is reproposed, and in these terms it is unclear how the connotative semiotic could also be subjected to "an analysis according to just the same procedure" as that valid for the denotative semiotic [Hjelmslev 1943: 119].

Moreover, it is no accident if still within Chapter 22, the opposition between a denotative semiotic on the one hand, and a connotative semiotic and a metasemiotic on the other, based on the operative terms *expression* and *content*, is viewed as inadequate and replaced by a new opposition between scientific semiotics and non-scientific semiotics, based on the concept of operation, previously defined as "a description that is in agreement with the empirical principle" [31]—that is, free of contradiction, exhaustive, and as simple as possible [11]: "By a *scientific semiotic* we mean a semiotic that is an operation; by a *non-scientific semiotic* we understand a semiotic that is not an operation. We accordingly define a *connotative semiotic* as a non-scientific semiotic one or more of whose planes is (are) (a) semiotic(s), and a *metasemiotic* as a scientific semiotic one or more of whose planes is (are) (a) semiotic(s). The case that usually occurs in practice is, as we have seen, that *one* of the planes is a semiotic" [120]. As the analysis proceeds, the concept of a denotative semiotic is completely reabsorbed, and the simplified model of "a semiotic none of whose planes is a semiotic" [114] gives way to the recognition of the object in all its complexity.

Connotation, therefore, is not a specific mark of literature; or better still, literary language cannot be opposed to standard language on the basis of it. Every text is necessarily connotative: denotation and connotation may be distinguished only as different moments in the analysis. This does not mean that the notion of connotation and, more precisely, that of connotator, cannot be applied to the theory and description of literary texts, as well as to that of every other textual manifestation. For the moment a small step forward could be made by overcoming the misleading opposition between denotative languages and connotative languages, which should be reformulated, at least in a provisional and problematic way, in terms of the opposition of the connotators of "standard" language to the specific connotators of the "literary" text. How far it would be useful and theoretically correct to isolate these latter will be seen later. Nor should particular cases of overlapping be excluded a priori. For example, a connotator representing a "familiar" style could in some cases be associated with connotators generally defined as "literary": versification, presence of rhyme or other phonic figures, and so on. Besides, when we speak of "dialectal poetry," "parodic poetry," "comic poetry," and the like, we are merely combining two connotators under the same label, one "literary" ("poetry"), the other not, since there are discourses that are not "poetic," "dialectal," "parodic," or "comic." Strictly literary connotation (or that presumed such) does not exclude other forms of connotation, present in standard or, in any case, nonliterary language. And vice versa: if I should call, ironically or with feigned affectation, the object with which I am writing a *stylus*, I would be using a term with strictly literary connotations, in contemporary English at least. And indeed, any dictionary provides some of its entries' connotators by resorting to standard abbreviations: *arch.* (archaic), *colloq.* (colloquial), *dial.* (dialectal), *fig.* (figurative), *iron.* (ironical), *joc.* (jocular), *liter.* (literary), *pejor.* (pejorative), *poet.* (poetic), *scient.* (scientific), *vulg.* (vulgar), and so on. It should be understood that I am using simple, schematic examples and that connotation obviously is not only concerned with the lexicon: the analysis can and must include all units in the text. Thus a text in which the connotator "literary" may be identified can then have the further connotation of "poetic" if it is in verse; a "poetic" text may be 'prosaic" if its style is close to that of prose, and its verse form may be "syllabic" ("regular" or "irregular"), or "anisosyllabic," or "free." Likewise, the connotator "archaic" may appear not only in the lexicon (*brethren* for *brothers*), or in the syntax (*What means this?* for *What does this mean?*), or in orthography (*draught* for *draft*), but also, for instance, in metrical style. The use of the sestina in a twentieth-century context (Pound, Ungaretti, Fortini) is an obvious archaism, as is also that of the so-called optional diaeresis and of other metrical figures beyond a certain date.

Clearly—and this does not contradict the above argument—literary texts may display specific phenomena of functionalization of connotation, though, it must be added, these are parallel to that which may also occur in nonliterary texts. According to Prieto, who is responsible for a number of important clarifications about the concept of connotation [1975: 66–77], the same may be said for all forms of artistic communication: "The artistic phenomenon, which is always a communicative phenomenon at the connotative level, may be so only at this level or, moreover, at the level of the basic operation. Now these two possibilities would seem to correspond to two fundamental forms of the artistic phenomenon: on the one hand we would have the arts that we may term 'literary,' that is, those where the basic operation is in itself a communicative operation, and which include literature of course, but also dance, the plastic figurative arts, cinema, theater, comic strips, etc.; and on the other hand, the arts that we may call 'architectural,' where the basic operation is not in itself a communicative operation, and whose domain would cover architecture and design" [72]. Finally, the "musical" arts, which include music, the nonfigurative plastic arts, and nonfigurative dance, may partially be assimilated to the literary arts, although they rest on a subjective and not an objective universe, that is to say, on the addressee's command of the specific code [72–73].

To apply, or rather to extend, Hjelmslev's theory to the study of literary texts reassigns the latter to the competence of the linguist, or more generally, of the semiotician, while providing important suggestions for the construction of unitary models of textual analysis. In the first place a text would be examined as a denotative semiotic, and at this stage of the analysis all the connotators of various degrees would be deducted. In a second moment (distinct but not necessarily successive moments in a chronological sense), the analysis would shift to the connotators themselves and to the functions they contract with the expression plane, consisting of the denotative semiotic. Of course, the problems of a formal analysis of the connotators still remain, and are the same as those present in the analysis of the content of a denotative semiotic: these will have to be faced and solved by future developments of linguistic theory. But even if it is too early yet to point to any operative solution in this direction, glossematics must be given the credit for having restored the text to linguistics, overcoming Saussure's *langue/parole* dichotomy and the assumption that linguistic science deals only with the *langue*. "For our present investigation, which is concerned with textual analysis," writes Hjelmslev, "it is the process and not the system that is of interest" [25]. This step forward is made possible precisely through the notion of connotative semiotic and by placing the language (*langue*) into a semiotic process that ultimately transcends it. It is only within the realm of a connotative semiotic that every communicative act, ordinary or literary, may be perceived and analyzed as a whole, be led back to the system it determines [39], but at the same time be observed in all its aspects and shades, which are intrinsic to communication. Finally, and this is what concerns us most, it appears incorrect to set up a priori distinctions in the treatment of "literary" and "nonliterary" texts other than those suggested on each occasion by their greater or lesser complexity and size.

It is now obvious that once we have dismissed the oversimplified identification of the connotative semiotic with literary language and attributed various forms of connotation to any text or linguistic act, the presence of connotators is no longer sufficient motive for classifying a text as "literary." Literary language and standard language are still terms lacking definition. In the analysis of connotative semiotics the question of a typology of "specifically" literary connotators cannot be considered until we move within a framework of a metasemiotic of connotative semiotics, a metasemiotic which, according to Hjelmslev, will require the contribution of "many special sciences, in the first place, presumably, sociology, ethnology and psychology" [125]. Such vague or very general indications seem to have little to do with literature, but they take on a new meaning for our problem, because it is at this point, and at this point alone, that the need arises to analyze the "content-purports" [125], that is, to refer to extralinguistic (historical, social, psychological, anthropological) phenomena. In practice, the notions of "literary," "poetic," and so on do not emerge from intrinsic qualities of the object, but may be defined only when confronted with a necessarily external reality, and by virtue of the social functioning of the text.

1

Standard Language and Literary Language

The misunderstanding and misuse of Hjelmslev's theory cannot be considered merely as an exegetic accident befalling a few literary semioticians. It is but one episode in a long tradition of studies, whose principal aim has been the search for literariness, that is, for linguistic properties that would make a given text a piece of literature.

Before going on, however, I feel the need to insert a terminological parenthesis in order to avoid possible confusion later. In twentieth-century critical languages, "poetic" and "literary" at times are synonyms; at others, they are used to refer to different literary genres ("poetic" being a marked term, denoting a form of literature composed in verse, while "literary" includes verse and prose); and at others still, they imply aesthetic considerations (poetry/nonpoetry). Moreover, there is a widespread belief that one may term "poetry" "that apparent prose, called poetic or art prose, whose characteristic is the parity of rights, the absolute equality given to sound and sense, to the signified and signifier—an equality that does not belong to the typology of prose as such" [Corti 1976: 69]—but, it must be added, only if one were to call "prose" that poetry which, through the author's intentions or lack of ability, appears to be defi-

13

cient on the side of the sound and the signifier. Nevertheless, these terminological overlappings have little or no practical advantages and leave an ambiguous boundary between both series of texts. In the following pages, quotations apart, the term "poetic" will refer exclusively to works in verse form, and will be made to coincide with "metrical" [Di Girolamo 1976: 102–10]; "prose" will be opposed to "poetry"; and "literature" will be used as an unmarked term, as well as one still to be defined.

The theory of the formal method was the first to pose the problem of a systematic definition of literary language. The interests of the Russian formalists, and later of the Prague School structuralists, as they themselves declared, did not lie so much in the nature of the aesthetic fact as in the functioning of literary works as such. In order to fulfill this aim the formalists avoided questions like, What is beauty? What is literature? and preferred instead to describe the specific characteristics of literary material, opposing the literary series to the nearest nonliterary series, that is, standard language.

As Èjxenbaum wrote in 1927, in his concise assessment of the formalists' activity from 1915 to 1925, "the organization of the formal method was governed by the principle that the study of literature should be made specific and concrete. . . . To establish this principle of specificity without resorting to speculative aesthetics required the juxtaposing of the literary order of facts with another such order. For this purpose one order had to be selected from among existent orders, which, while contiguous with the literary order, would contrast with it in terms of functions. It was just such a methodological procedure that produced the opposition between 'poetic' language and 'practical' language. This opposition was set forth in the first *Opojaz* publications . . . and it served as the activating principle for the formalists' treatment of the fundamental problems of poetics" [1927*a*: 7–8].

The founders of the Prague Linguistic Circle adopted these same directions with a number of corrections, but also with a more rigid attitude over some points. Jan Mukařovský provided one of the most explicit definitions of the relationship between standard language and poetic language from the Prague viewpoint. The question, according to Mukařovský, can be put in these terms: "What is the *relationship* between the extension of *poetic language* and that of the *standard*, between the places of each in the total system of the whole of language? Is poetic language a special brand of the standard, or is it an independent formation? Poetic language cannot be called a brand of the standard, if for no other reason than that poetic language has at its disposal, from the standpoint of lexicon, syntax, etc., all the forms of the given language—often of different developmental stages thereof. . . . Poetic language is thus not a brand of the standard. This is not to deny the close connection between the two, which consists in the fact that, for poetry, the standard language is the background against which is reflected the aesthetically intentional distortion of the linguistic components of the work; in other words, the intentional violation of the norm of the standard. . . . The violation of the norm of the standard, its systematic violation, is what makes possible the poetic utilization of language; without this possibility there would be no poetry. The more the norm of the standard is stabilized in a given language, the more varied can be its violation, and therefore the more possibilities for poetry in that language. And on the other hand, the weaker the awareness of this norm, the fewer possibilities of violation, and hence the fewer possibilities for poetry" [1932: 17–18].

Slavic formalism, therefore, defines literary language in terms of a deviation from standard language, thus giving rise to one of the most successful and recurrent concepts of twentieth-century critical theories. From an operative viewpoint, this notion has had the merit of emphasizing the literary work as an "artifice" (a "pure" linguistic artifice, existing for its own sake; or, according to Šklovskij [1929], an artifice whose aim is estrangement), concentrating the critic's attention on the message itself rather than on the moral, psychological, and sociological implications, which, despite their possible importance, cannot ever qualify a text as literary. This principle is formulated clearly by Jakobson when he writes that "the object of the science of literature is not literature but literariness, in other words, that which makes a specific work a literary work" [1921: 11].

Nevertheless, from a theoretical standpoint, the concept of "deviation" (or "écart," as others will say, using Valéry's expression) reveals several weaknesses.

First, as has often been observed, not all deviations constitute in themselves a "literary" connotator. Thus, an ungrammatical sentence is not automatically poetic, even if many have identified in a famous example of a grammatically deviant sentence, *colorless green ideas sleep furiously*, specific poetic qualities due perhaps to the author's hidden creative gifts. Yet one must agree that not all the grammatical "errors" produced by a schoolboy, for instance, have poetic aims and effects, while some literary texts have a very low level of deviation, or even none at all. Moreover, as Trubeckoj remarked in 1924 in his review of a book by Jakobson on versification, there is a clear limit to language's patience. An answer to this objection comes from the latest developments of this school, which we shall term "deviationist" along with Fish [1973–74]. Bierwisch [1965], for example, refers to "rules of deviation": grammatical irregularities achieve poetic effect only when they cease being mere violations of language and acquire instead their own specific regularity; while Lotman [1970] speaks of literary language as a secondary system built over the natural language. Despite these adjustments, some doubt still remains as to the validity of the contrastive procedure in providing a definition of literary language.

Obviously, poetry may be defined in relation to that which is not poetry—that is, prose, or rather art prose. In this way homogeneous elements are confronted, and it is easier to underline particular forms of tension (of a prosodic kind, for example) between a text in verse and one in prose. Likewise, one may describe Italian courtly poetry by comparing it to Provençal; Marinistic lyric, by comparing it to the Petrarchist tradition; and so on. The method is almost algebraic: the sum of the new elements with respect to a specific object taken as a point of comparison, and the subtraction of the missing elements. The same method may be applied also to individuals (Petrarch's language compared to Dante's), and even outside of literature (contrastive methods of language teaching).

Nevertheless, a few basic conditions are necessary for this kind of contrastive procedure to have some sense, or to be methodologically correct. First of all, the comparison must be carried out following a principle of economy—that is, by confronting structures or systems that are close to each other or, better still, contiguous. One may compare a poet's style to that of his contemporaries or immediate precursors, but there would be little to gain, even though it is theoretically possible, in comparing the English of a "man in the street" of our day to the English of William Shakespeare. A further condition is that the comparison be between homogeneous elements, such as two systems or two texts, or between parts of two systems or two texts. All of this might seem obvious and trivial, as indeed it is, but very few people have asked themselves whether a definition of literary language as opposed to standard language fulfills the minimum conditions necessary for this type of analysis.

To oppose literary language to standard language actually means opposing nonhomogeneous elements, even though the two sets may be considered contiguous. When one compares the linguistic "deviations" in a text, one is comparing the literary *parole* to the standard *langue*, while the only correct comparison is between *langues* (Italian and English) or between *paroles* (Petrarch and Dante). The deviationists do claim to refer to the literary "system," but the confrontation does not usually take place between the standard system and the literary system, difficult or impossible to define, but between the (literary) text and the standard language. Moreover, one cannot really speak of a "system of deviations" unless "deviation" is given the meaning, as suggested by Saporta [1960: 92], of "additional restrictions beyond those of the general grammar" (for example, rhyme, meter, rhythm). Yet these restrictions normally involve individual genres or subgenres, and therefore may be explained within the series itself, without the need for recourse to a comparison to the extraliterary series. To oppose the literary *parole* to the standard *langue* is as meaningful as to define the standard *parole* as deviant with respect to the literary *langue*; there will be obvious differences in both cases. Every text, every act of *parole* (oral or written), contains a certain degree of deviation (in the pronunciation, lexicon, syntax, etc.) from the language's ideal code. Otherwise the language of the man in the street, like that of Shakespeare, would be grammar tout court; and the fundamental distinction of structural linguistics between *langue* and *parole*, system and process, phoneme and sound, would be meaningless.

It is almost impossible to distinguish the observable and possible deviations of spoken language from the "specific" deviations of the literary text. In fact, in a diachronic perspective, the formalist theory of literature's evolving by sudden changes, proposed in the first place by Tynjanov [1929*a*], may be verified in the history of languages. When, in Vulgar Latin, *blancu* was first used instead of *albu*, it must have seemed a "deviation" until *blancu* definitely became part of the system, replacing *albu*, which must have been perceived as an archaism for some time before disappearing altogether. And in fact, the close ties between the theory of literary evolution and the new linguistic views on diachrony developing in the late twenties (Jakobson, Trubeckoj) are well-documented (see, for example, the essay by Tynjanov and Jakobson [1928] on the "study of literature and language").

With this, I am not attempting to make any paradoxical claims. It is only common sense to note that the language of this essay, for instance, differs in various aspects from that of a poem, even a contemporary one; or that a letter to a friend follows quite different "rules" from those of a novel, even from a strictly linguistic standpoint. Modern linguistics, especially sociolinguistics, has taught us to recognize a plurality of levels in language, always (and justly) avoiding pointing out which is the "right" or "correct" level. The question is rather another: Can one really speak of standard language and literary language as linguistic entities that can be recognized and isolated accurately within a stratification which is extremely dense and allows for continuous exchanges between levels? To arbitrarily isolate two poles that are obviously different, ignoring any intermediate nuances, is to underestimate the complexity of language, as well as that of literary language.

More important still is the fact that "standard language," the term essential to the opposition, is as yet undefined. The comparison would be meaningful only if, to return to Hjelmslev's terminology, one could admit the existence of an uncontaminated denotative semiotic, a degree zero of language in which grammar would be synonymous with style, a language neutral in every one of its manifestations, univocal and colorless. But nobody believes that such a (natural) language exists, has ever existed, or could ever exist; and one is left with the feeling that "standard language" represents a kind of instrumental phantom to be called upon and opposed to "literary language." In short, the standard is defined as a nonliterary language, but neither standard language nor, consequently, literary language are ever defined. "Attempting to distinguish literature from nonliterature at the level of the *langue*," writes Mary Louise Pratt, criticizing the "'poetic language' fallacy," "has the effect of locating the concerns of poetics outside those of general linguistics, while retaining an analogy between the two disciplines allows the disparity of their aims to remain hidden behind a uniformity of terminology and method. It is this separation of powers that, I believe, 'ordinary language' as a linguistic construct was invented to support" [1977: 15–16].

Indeed, to base the definition of literary language on the opposition to the standard involves an implicit division of labor and a mutual exclusion of the critic's and the linguist's methodologies. This might seem paradoxical considering the fact that contemporary criticism owes so much to Saussurian and post-Saussurian linguistics, and that some of the foremost linguists of our century have practiced literary analysis, while the opposite does not seem to have occurred. Yet, inevitably, all deviationist theories eventually give up the strictly linguistic approach, while preserving at most an ever more empty terminological apparatus.

Stanley Fish clearly sums up the problem's salient points. "Linguists resolutely maintain that literature is, after all, language, and that therefore a linguistic description of a text is necessarily relevant to the critical act; critics just as resolutely maintain that linguistic analyses leave out something, and that what they leave out is precisely what constitutes literature. This leads to an attempt, undertaken sometimes by one part, sometimes by the other, to identify the formal properties peculiar to literary texts, an attempt that inevitably fails when, either the properties so identified turn out to be found in texts not considered literary, or when obviously literary texts do not display the specified properties. In the end, neither side has victory, but each can point to the other's failure: the critics have failed to provide an objective criterion for the asserted uniqueness of their subject matter; the linguists have failed to provide the kind of practical demonstration that would support the claims they make for their discipline and its apparatus" [1973–74: 41]. Fish's proposed solution consists in overcoming the opposition between literary language and standard language, and looking instead "to the more interesting, because it is more liberating, conclusion that *there is no such thing as ordinary language*" [49], at least not in the current sense of a haven for all rules and norms.

The blissful idyll between linguistics and criticism has thus been tainted because of the historically motivated tendency of all or almost all of structural linguistics to become a science of the *langue*, relegating the study of the *parole* to a secondary position. This was already clear in Saussure [1916: 17–20], and in 1965 Chomsky still maintained that linguistic theory "is concerned primarily with an ideal speaker-listener, in a completely homogeneous speech-community, who knows its language perfectly and is unaffected by such grammatically irrelevant conditions as memory limitations, distractions, shifts of attention and interest, and errors (random or characteristic) in applying his knowledge of language in actual performance" [1965: 3]. As we have seen, only the theoretical model put forward by Hjelmslev [1941; 1943] opens the way to a linguistics that in the final analysis faces the text in its uniqueness and irrepeatability, thereby taking into account that "variety of factors" which Chomsky, following the founders of modern linguistics, preliminarily excluded, and which the critics are ready, rightly enough, to claim within their competence.

2

Uses and Functions of Language

A less schematic approach to our problem consists in identifying different functions in language.

In an early formulation of this theory, some formalists opposed a practical to an aesthetic function of language. This distinction may seem an immediate reflection of the opposition between standard language and literary language; but it is also reminiscent of the terms already diffused by Italian neo-idealism. Significantly, it reappears in the glossematic milieu, where Stender-Petersen [1949: 279], in his quest for pure beauty, goes as far as to exclude architecture, "a secondary, applied art," from the three fine arts—music, the plastic arts (painting and sculpture), and literature—thus confirming the fact that this must have been a deep-rooted notion in twentieth-century (non-marxist) aesthetics. It is no accident that this opposition arose at a time and in an ideological context in which art was no longer required to have cognitive or didactic aims, and when the producers and consumers of works of art spoke of the complete autonomy of aesthetics. Poetry is entirely "useless," said Oscar Wilde; and the slogan "art for art's sake" had already been coined.

In their classic "study of the influence of language upon thought and of the science of symbolism," Ogden and Richards [1923] had singled out five functions of language that may be summed up in a "symbolic use" and an "emotive use" of signs. This bipolar opposition (despite some terminological fluctuations) gave new vitality to the discussion already begun by the early formalists. In 1932, Mukařovský still defined the poetic function of language as the "foregrounding" (*aktualisace* in the original) of the utterance. "Foregrounding is the opposite of automatization, that is the de-automatization of an act; the more an act is automatic, the less it is consciously executed; the more it is foregrounded, the more completely conscious does it become. . . . In poetic language foregrounding achieves maximum intensity to the extent of pushing communication into the background as the objective of expression and of being used for its own sake; it is not used in the services of communication, but in order to place in the foreground the act of expression, the act of speech itself" [1932: 19]. Poetry, therefore, is the opposite of communication.

Although the contrast may seem clear-cut in theory, in critical practice the formalists were much less categorical about recognizing the limits between one function and the other. In the later years of the movement, for example, the formalists began to study "documentary literature"—diaries, autobiography, reportage.

Instructive, and at the same time singular, is Jakobson's discussion on the Czech poet Mácha. Mácha left some romantically inspired poetry and prose which describe his love for a woman, Lori, in an exalted and delicate tone; but he also left a diary, published posthumously, which tells the same story in its carnal aspects with all sorts of obscenities. "In his diary, Mácha, the lyric poet, depicts his physiological, erotic, and excremental functions in a clearly epic manner. With an accountant's inexorable precision, he jots down in a tedious code, how and how often he has satisfied his desire during his meetings with Lori" [1933–34: 132]. Jakobson's intention is to dispel any determining relationship between *Dichtung* and *Wahrheit*, between art and life; and indeed, he maintains that both versions of the story are equally true, though described in different modes and styles: it is merely a question of two semantic levels of the same object, the same experience. What is interesting for our purposes is that Jakobson considers the diary literature, or poetry, since it appears devoid of any "utilitarian" aims: we are in the presence of "art for art's sake," he writes, adding that if Mácha had lived in another age and had been called Joyce or Lawrence, he would have published the diary and kept his lyric poems locked in a closet [133]. Thus, according to Jakobson, a literary work is not defined by the possibility of its being accepted as such by its audience (by its "publicability"), but by intrinsic qualities distinguishing it from nonliterary works. Even a personal diary may be taken as literature once the presence of these intrinsic qualities has been ascertained.

At this point we may observe that the opposition is no longer between literary language (meaning a system of rules and institutions of writing) and standard language (all that is not literary language), but rather between a so-called aesthetic function and a so-called practical or referential function of language. "Poetry is language in its aesthetic function," Jakobson had already postulated in 1921 [11]. But this means that the aesthetic function may also be present in ordinary language, since it is difficult to view a diary as a work referring to a literary "system." Mácha's journal did not fit into any genre or trend existing in his day, both because of its obscene contents and the equally obscene way in which these were expressed: no reader would have taken it for literature, and it is only by chance that the change in the literary institutions some time later allowed for such works to be produced and accepted as literature.

More complex is Jakobson's treatment of linguistic functions in his classic paper [1960] read at the Bloomington Conference on Style in 1958: a much more articulate classification now replaces the head-on opposition between literary and nonliterary language, or between aesthetic and referential function.

Besides Ogden and Richards's emotive and symbolic (or referential) functions, Jakobson identifies in language a conative function, derived from Bühler [1933], a phatic function, isolated by Malinowsky [1923], and a metalingual function, originating with the Polish logicians and Carnap [1934]; finally, as an autonomous function, he adds the poetic function. Every function may be distinguished as prevalently oriented toward one of the six essential factors of verbal communication, schematized as follows:

CONTEXT

ADDRESSER   MESSAGE   ADDRESSEE
          – – – – – – – – – – – – – –
CONTACT

CODE

The emotive function expresses the speaker's attitude toward that about which he is speaking, and is focused on the addresser: it is found in an almost pure state in interjections. The conative function, represented by the imperative and vocative, is oriented toward the addressee. The phatic function is the set for contact, the testing of the channel (a *hello* on the telephone, or *are you listening?*, etc.); the referential function is directed toward the context (an animate or inanimate "third person"); and the metalingual function is realized when focus is on the code, on language itself. Finally, in Jakobson's words, the poetic function is "the set (*Einstellung*) toward the message as such, focus on the message for its own sake" [1960: 356]. Thus the scheme of the factors at play in every act of verbal communication may be compared to the scheme of the six functions of language:

REFERENTIAL

EMOTIVE   POETIC   CONATIVE

PHATIC

METALINGUAL

In recent years, the theory of linguistic functions has been taken up and expanded from slightly different viewpoints and according to the particular methodological and disciplinary concerns of the individual authors. One could mention, for instance, the ethnologist Hymes [1962; 1964; 1973–74] and the linguists Rosiello [1965: 45–114] and Halliday [1970; 1971].

More original, even though traceable to the same theoretical background, is Zumthor's approach, based on medieval examples. Zumthor distinguishes, by virtue of the "property of message" of the discourse, between "linguistic *monuments* (the Strasburg Oaths; the oral formula used customarily by a judge) and *documents* (any sentence of everyday communication; the notes in the sermon on Jonah). . . . As a general rule, in any linguistic community one may distinguish: 1) a primary, 'documentary' state of language, with a basically communicative function; 2) a secondary, 'monumentary' state, existing in relation to the former but irreducible to it. A functional distinction: we shall refer to a 'primary function' and a 'secondary function' of language, expressions which are questionable in theory, but which in practice are extremely useful. The *primary function* is determined merely by the needs of current intercommunication; the *secondary function* is a real 'edifying' function, in the two senses of the word: moral elevation and construction of an edifice. . . . On the one hand, the speaker expresses himself in his subjectivity, in the immediacy of his experience (primary function); on the other, he sometimes requires language to universalize this experience (secondary function)" [1963: 32–33]. Nevertheless, though this distinction is partly justified by the desire to add some perspective to a landscape that the philological method often tends to flatten, it still seems extremely schematic and rigid. It would be hard to attribute an intent to universalize experience to the Strasburg Oaths (monumentary or secondary function), while this might easily be present in an unregistered or unregisterable linguistic act, expressed within the speaker's "subjectivity." The "monument" (juridical or even legislative—an edict, for instance) may have specific practical aims (the individual's behavior within society), thereby serving (inter)communication; yet not all the aspects of the spoken language, employed in the "immediacy" of one's experience, aim at "everyday intercommunication," and it would be impossible to monumentalize, for example, any product of Jakobson's emotive function, such as interjections.

In 1975, Zumthor returned to the subject, restating it with the aid of a more solid theoretical apparatus and referring to Jakobson (who was only fleetingly mentioned in the 1963 book). The "birth" of a literature in a new idiom is viewed as the affirmation of the poetic, or, using Halliday's term, "textual," function, and it therefore reflects a community's becoming aware of its own language. "As soon as this consciousness attains a certain point of clarity, language thinks itself, exists objectively and thereby postulates and actualizes a need for universalization and for historicization which constitutes, in one form or another, the literary *fait*" [1975: 206]. This is an hypothesis that is stimulating in itself, but one hesitates to support it because of the extremely restrictive definition Zumthor still gives of literature: "'Literature' will . . . appear . . . as a class of expressions in which, even if all the other functions come into play, the unity and the specific quality of the expressions reside in the particular strength which is given to the textual function, as a result of a concentration of the message, as form, upon itself. . . . The 'literary' text will therefore include an interiorization of the referent, whence (secondarily) a predominance of connotation over denotation, of emotion over designation" [203]. And here it is clear that, apart from a further abuse of Hjelmslev's terminology, the 1963 distinctions are being reproposed beneath a new veneer.

More decisively oriented toward a revision of Jakobson's theorem, though still tied to the referential/nonreferential opposition, is Maria Corti's suggestion [1976: 89] of the notion of the literary text as a "hypersign" (based on Eco [1976: 261–76]), or as a message loaded with a sign superfunction, that is, fulfilled in the confrontation with the addressees: "So it seems that the argument that poetic language communicates only itself, does not exhaust the question; it is valid only in that poetic language is autonomous with respect to its referents, that is, on the level of a primal semantics or the semantics of ordinary language. More precisely, the poetic text emits a message that changes the grammar of vision of its readers in the face of reality" [80]. On the other hand, Corti herself seems to be reproposing the question in substantialistic terms when, in her criticism of Jakobson, she wonders where to situate "the qualitative difference between the application of the poetic function in language and the poetic language of a text," and then distinguishes between "texts . . . that are formally poetic," such as advertisements, where there is "a strong and informed use of the poetic function of language" but in which "there is no poetry," and the "true poetic text" (which seems to mean "not formally but substantially poetic") [78]. But unless the discussion shifts to the aesthetic plane—that is, to the plane of the difference between a "good" poem and a "bad" poem—these distinctions, though presented as objective, lack any real foundation and any possibility of being verified. Of no help either is the reference [50–52] to van Dijk's hypothesis of a grammar of the literary system [1972*b*], which is said to contain additional rules compared to general textual grammar (rhyme, alliteration, a specific lexicon, etc.), because there is nothing to prevent these rules from appearing, for instance, even in an advertisement.

Despite these (and other) fluctuations, Jakobson's model represents the clearest, almost classic formulation of the theory of linguistic functions, and also stands as a synthesis of a debate that has lasted over half a century. Thus it is to Jakobson that we shall have to turn to pick up the threads of our investigation.

3

The Dominant

Jakobson maintains that "the linguistic study of the poetic function must overstep the limits of poetry," while "the linguistic scrutiny of poetry cannot limit itself to the poetic function" [1960: 357]. The poetic function, therefore, may be present in the political slogan, in the advertisement, in everyday speech; while other functions of language may possibly appear in poetry stricto sensu: in fact, "any attempt to reduce the sphere of poetic function to poetry or confine poetry to poetic function would be a delusive oversimplification" [356].

Jakobson's definition of the poetic function, however, cannot easily be made to fit prose. If the essence of poetry lies in the "continuous parallelism" and in the repetition of the same "figure of sound," to use Hopkins's terms, then clearly the poetic function is present primarily in verse; and if "verse always implies poetic function" [359], then one may overturn the statement and claim that poetic function always implies verse ("verse" in the broad sense, meaning a reiterated phonic figure, and not necessarily a codified metrical system). On the contrary, in prose "parallelisms are not so strictly marked and strictly regular as 'continuous parallelism' and . . . there is no dominant figure of sound"; prose, therefore, presents

"more entangled problems for poetics, as does any transitional linguistic area. In this case the transition is between strictly poetic and
strictly referential language" [374]. Thus, curiously, though coher-
ently with respect to the above premises, art prose, while still constituting an object of poetics, occupies a peripheral position in the
poetic function and is qualified as a transitional linguistic area in the
direction of the referential function. It is not clear, however, why in
prose this transition cannot also occur between "strictly poetic"
function and all the other functions of language. A diary is, in fact,
aimed at the addresser (emotive function), a correspondence or an
epistolary novel at the addressee (conative function), and there is no
lack either of literary occurrences of the phatic function, aimed at
the contact (Jakobson himself provides some examples [188–89]),
and of the metalingual function, aimed at the code (one could mention the outline of the *Dictionnaire des idées reçues* that should have
concluded *Bouvard et Pécuchet*, or the many examples to be found
in the works of Gadda).

Jakobson does indeed refer to Propp's pioneering work on the
Russian folktale [1928] and to Levi-Strauss's more recent contribu-
tions [1958–59; 1960] as examples of a "syntactic" approach to narrative structures; yet it is quite clear that, even if one were to admit
the universal applicability of this procedure, Jakobson's definition of
the poetic function is too rigid, leaving prose poised between one
box and another in the scheme of functions.

But, there is a further complication. One should not confuse prose
and narrative, for there are forms of verse narrative, such as epic,
medieval romance, and narrative poems. In these cases a sum of the
figures occurs—figures of sound and figures of narration—and it
would be unjustified to privilege the metrical over the narrative
level.

It is common knowledge that prose usually appears later than poetry and that some literatures have a remarkable poetic patrimony,
yet have never known prose. From a certain point of view [Frye
1963; *EPP*, s.v. "Verse and prose"], poetry would actually be closer
to the spontaneous, control-free language of children and unedu-
cated adults than prose; and if poetry has its rules and restrictions
(meter, rhyme, alliteration, etc.), the same may be said of prose,
which follows equally rigid, or in some respects even more com-

plex, rules that almost entirely elude the dominion of poetics in Jakobson's sense. On the other hand, the difference between poetry and prose, which may be dealt with at a theoretical level using the contrastive method (particularly effective here), should not conceal the fact that the choice of either one or the other depends on the development of the literary genres, on the audience's taste, on the medium selected (oral performance or written diffusion), and on many other factors. There are no contents naturally destined to poetry, nor contents naturally destined to prose. Genres that seem predominantly prosaic to us, like the novel and the novella, originated in medieval poetic genres like courtly romance, the lai, and the fabliau. In more recent times. lyric itself has been translated into prose in the *poème en prose*, often giving rise to the (sometimes satisfied) embarrassment of many theorists. Thus, to follow Jakobson and isolate the poetics of prose from that of poetry, employing two different gauges, means to divide arbitrarily a phenomenon that is substantially unitary.

At this point, the notion of literature almost disappears entirely, together, perhaps, with that of literariness: the electoral slogan *I like Ike* or the verse advertisement of any detergent is closer to the *Commedia*, from the standpoint of poetics, than either *Moby Dick* or *Madame Bovary*. Naturally I do not say this for the sake of scandal: and indeed, it is interesting to observe the evolution of a poetician who was once one of the major exponents of the formal method, and who now goes so far as to eliminate any fundamental difference between the language of poetry and ordinary language. Jakobson, however, remains entirely consistent with his point of departure in defining poetry as a message aimed at itself and in identifying its essence in its nonreferential quality.

Even if we leave aside those literary genres that, in this view, are relegated to a kind of no-man's-land, some problems remain. As we have already seen, Jakobson does not deny the presence in true poetry of other functions in a subordinate position, alongside the dominant poetic function; and, contrariwise, of the poetic function even in nonpoetic utterances. This reintroduces the notion of the "dominant," already attested (especially with reference to the theory of genres) in Tomaševskij [1928] and in Tynjanov [1929a] and later taken up again by Jakobson in 1935 in an important lecture. Here he claims that "the dominant may be defined as the focusing component of a work of art: it rules, determines, and transforms the remaining components" [1935a: 82]; thus "a poetic work cannot be defined as a work fulfilling neither an exclusively aesthetic function nor an aesthetic function along with other functions; rather, a poetic work is defined as a verbal message whose aesthetic function is its dominant" [84]. The same concept reappears in 1958: "Poetic function is not the sole function of verbal art but only its dominant, determining function, whereas in all other verbal activities it acts as a subsidiary, accessory constituent" [1960: 356].

A dominant element then, but for whom? On the basis of which criteria may we consider the poetic function in the slogan *I like Ike* as "secondary", and as "primary" or "dominant" in works to which we do not now begrudge the label of poetry? One need only think of a few examples, to which every reader may add his own. One wonders, for instance, which linguistic function is dominant in the oldest Castilian epics, where the referential function seems to have been so important as to lead the historiographers of Alfonso el Sabio's *Primera Crónica General* to turn them into prose and, in some cases, to transcribe them almost literally, so that Menéndez Pidal believed he could "reconstruct" some hundred lines of the *Siete Infantes de Lara* from the chronicle. Another significant example is that of Gonzalo de Berceo's *Vida de San Millán*. In this poem the author, a notary from the monastery of San Millán de la Cogolla in Rioja, gives particular emphasis to a posthumous miracle in which San Millán appears in the sky, together with Santiago, during a battle against the Moors, thus putting the enemy to flight. As a sign of gratitude, tributes were to be paid regularly to the monasteries of Santiago and San Millán. During the thirteenth century, a Latin decree ordering these tributes and said to have been made by Fernán González, Count of Castile and one of the battle's protagonists, turned up in the archives at San Millán: this was not another miracle, but almost certainly an apocryphal document in whose drafting Berceo himself might have had a hand; and, indeed, his *Vida de San Millán*, written at about the same time, suspiciously culminates in the same episode. Thus there is a considerable affinity between the apocryphal document and the poem, both of them having the same "function" of asking for money, and it would be difficult to maintain, therefore, that the message of this poetic text exists for its own sake. Still on the Spanish scene, how should the political propaganda ballads for and against Pedro in the Trastámaran wars be qualified? Or, what should one say of Rutebeuf's poems against the mendicant friars' being admitted into the University of Paris? Edmond Faral believed that the poet was probably paid to turn the secular masters' polemical writings into verse. Depending on the tastes and literary institutions in force, propaganda may be condensed into a lively ballad, a lengthy epic, or even into the sophisticated, almost hermetic slogan printed on the campaign buttons for Eisenhower's election.

I have attempted to draw these few, and certainly not isolated, examples from medieval poetry, because its "formalism" has become almost a topos for some critics; it would be much easier to add modern examples, taken from poetics which qualify themselves principally on the basis of their "contents." At this point, can we feel so sure about defining the poetic function in *I like Ike* as secondary? Contrariwise, should lyric, epic, and hagiographic poetry be lowered to the level of an advertising slogan? How should we classify the *Internationale*, or some of Brecht's poems? What about nineteenth-century songs of national independence? Which linguistic function is dominant in Lucretius's *De rerum natura*, or even in Dante's *Commedia*?

The dominant, therefore, would have to be singled out either on a purely subjective basis or on that of the text's content, which would be unacceptable to a theorist such as Jakobson and would seem almost like a reproposal of the normative poetics of the past. Moreover, it is also difficult to exclude estimative and achronic attitudes that should be carefully avoided.

A verse advertisement may well disgust the aesthetic sensibility of any consumer of poetry and goods, but this is no reason to ignore its "poetic function," which may even be considered, if one accepts Jakobson's reasoning for a moment, as quantitatively "dominant" and not subordinated to other functions. In some advanced consumer societies, we are beginning to notice a greater emphasis on the context than on the advertised product itself, which may not even be described: this is the case with IBM's publicity in Italy, for example, while in the United States the multinational oil companies avoid mentioning the word *gas*, concentrating instead, in a more or less inspired manner, on topics of ecology or the exploitation of national energy resources. Thus the premises exist, as well as some examples, for a type of publicity where the referential and the conative functions are almost entirely lacking. And this is not to mention the cases in which advertising products of the past may be reproposed as artistic objects. This phenomenon is most noticeable in the figurative area: art-deco posters, old Coca-Cola advertisements, department store catalogs of a hundred years ago are now presented as having no utilitarian ends and offered for a purely "aesthetic" consumption. To introduce discriminations based on aesthetic value only complicates matters without solving the problem, for the judgements of "beauty" and "ugliness" may clearly also apply to a chivalresque poem or a sonnet, to which no one would deny the (technical) attribute of poetry. Even in the area of aesthetic theory, "the distinction . . . drawn between the aesthetic and the nonaesthetic is independent of all considerations of aesthetic value. . . . An abominable performance of the *London Symphony* is as aesthetic as a superb one; and Piero's *Risen Christ* is no more aesthetic but only better than a hack's. The symptoms of the aesthetic are not marks of merit; and a characterization of the aesthetic neither requires nor provides a definition of aesthetic excellence" [Goodman 1968: 255].

Furthermore, if we today can keep our distance in reading medieval verse encyclopedias and appreciate their poetry, we have no right to ignore completely that they were once vehicles of culture and science, no less than the latest issue of *Scientific American* might be to us. Nevertheless, the referential function in these and in so many other works of the past seems pale and blurred on reaching us, and we can then easily focus on the poetic function, which may be taken for the dominant even when it originally was not. It must be admitted, however, that the opposite procedure, of restoring a work's referentiality, is not always possible nor easy, since a whole series of information (historical, biographical, etc.) may escape us. At this point, any critical operation on a text or decision whether to include it in a history of literature would depend on the previous recognition of its dominant function.

In conclusion, one cannot really say that in this case Jakobson's analysis offers a solution to our problem. The attribute of "poetic" may be applied to any form of discourse, while art prose remains in a kind of limbo, with one foot inside and one outside the sacred grove. "True" poetry stands out from other forms of applied verse because of the predominance of the poetic function, but we have observed that the identification of the dominant inevitably turns into a subjective and frequently problematic operation. As for the other mark of poetry, the lack of any utilitarian aims, this might be the case of Mácha's diary, a text Jakobson considers on the borders of "literature," but it is certainly not true of a large number of works whose literariness has never been questioned. The price of Jakobson's theory is to split the corpus of literary works vertically and, when taken to its extreme consequences, to set up an arbitrary and unacceptable scale of poeticality.

4

The Role of the Audience

Curiously, one must again look back to the formalists for suggestions on the definition of literature in historical and sociological terms. These adjectives might seem rather too categorical and in contradiction with the formal method's well-known premises: yet, beyond the polemical distortions effected by some of the movement's critics, both the Russian formalists and, more explicitly still, the Prague structuralists viewed the literary work as an eminently social fact, though sui generis. Šklovskij's notion of estrangement, for example, or Mukařovský's concepts of norm and value would be inoperative without constant reference to an addressee. Furthermore, we have already noted how formalism attempted to give a functional, and not a substantial, definition of literature, even though I expressed doubts as to the real validity of a definition based on the opposition between literary language and standard language. Looking at the question from a different angle, however, and employing a fair amount of temporary schematization, one may admit, along with Tynjanov, that in each individual epoch, and within a homogeneous culture, the difference between literary and nonliterary is quite clear. "The very existence of a fact *as literary*," Tynjanov writes, "depends on its differential quality, that is, on its interrelationship with both literary and extraliterary orders. Thus, its existence depends on its function. What in one epoch would be a literary fact would in another be a common matter of social communication, and vice versa, depending on the whole literary system in which the given fact appears" [Tynjanov 1929*a*: 69]. Thus, the system of the literary order "is first of all a *system of the functions of the literary order which are in continual interrelationship with other orders*" [72].

Although this perspective honestly recognizes the relativeness of any definition of literature, it eventually seems to give up what Jakobson believed should be the formal method's principal task, that is, to grasp literariness. In order to identify the literary, one would theoretically have to refer to the aesthetic conceptions dominant in a specific age (though these may not always be reconstructed perfectly), with a rather embarrassing recourse, considering the premises, to the aid of the historian of culture. Moreover, one really does not know what to do about works (like Mácha's diary) that have only later become literary objects. Paradoxically, the formal analysis could get under way only after we have been informed from other sources, and not by the text itself, that a work is a literary work.

A similar outlook is adopted by Medvedev, an exponent, together with Baxtin and Vološinov, of the "sociological method" and a critic of the formal method, although he places greater emphasis on the text's ideological components. According to Medvedev, "the work absorbs and makes intrinsic to itself some elements of the ideological milieu, while rejecting other elements as extrinsic. Therefore the 'intrinsic' and the 'extrinsic' in the process of history dialectically change places without, needless to say, remaining absolutely identical at all the while. What appears today a fact extrinsic to literature—a piece of extraliterary reality—may tomorrow enter literature as one of its intrinsic structural factors. And conversely, what was literary today may become a piece of extraliterary reality tomorrow" [Medvedev 1928: 206, in Titunik 1973: 185].

Theoretically, an awareness of an epoch's system of values should help us place a work in its historical context and evaluate it in all its characteristics and peculiarities. When applied literally, however, this procedure becomes sociology of literature tout court, within which the scholar may only ascertain past taste and perhaps various kinds of aesthetic responses, which may not always be his own. If one concentrates exclusively on the audience's literary consciousness, any text's literariness will have to be redefined for each age; and clearly, here the only surviving "system" is that of the addressee's taste. Consequently, any attempt to found a general definition of the "literary" on the audience is destined to fail.

According to John Ellis, a text becomes literary only at the moment in which it is "used" as literature within a community of readers, that is, only when "the text is not taken as specifically relevant to the immediate context of its origin" [1974: 44]. To restore the text to its original context, as occurs in biographical, psychological, or ideological approaches, means in fact to reduce it to the level of a mere document. The proof of a text's literariness, in Ellis's view, rests instead on its being "relevant" to an audience, beyond its geographical and historical bounds or the specific circumstances in which it was produced. Neither the author's intentions, nor even his conforming to rigid canonical patterns (genres, styles, versification, etc.), suffice to qualify a work as literary. Likewise, it would be a mistake to study as literature texts of the past that have been completely forgotten, unless these are resurrected as literary texts in their own right through a renewed social circulation. Nevertheless, the weak point in Ellis's theory consists in the vagueness of his concept of community, which ends up by becoming an abstraction or, worse still, an indiscriminate sum of very different components. For a work to be considered literary, Ellis says, "the issues raised in the text must be thought of as relevant throughout the community: that is why they are found in the community's literary texts" [151]; but any sociologist knows how changeable and problematic the concept of audience can be, depending on the various epochs and, at the synchronic level, on the different social and cultural strata. Taking a text that very few people would be ready to define as nonliterary, the *Chanson de Roland* for example, one wonders how far the values it expresses were relevant to the whole of late-eleventh-century French society, or if they were not, rather, relevant to a fairly small section of that society. In other cases, every social group has its own literary works (handed down even beyond their original context), which express different values: no matter if these emanate spontaneously or are imposed by the dominant group. Furthermore, Ellis maintains that "if [the issues raised] are thought of primarily as the experience

of another age, to which a modern reader is an onlooker, then by
definition, the texts concerned are being treated not as the literary
texts of his culture at all, but only as historical documents and the
property of a culture foreign to him" [151–52]. Since any modern
reader of the *Chanson de Roland* would have little trouble in feeling
himself to be "an onlooker of the experiences of another age" and in
recognizing that culture as essentially foreign to him, one should
conclude that the *Chanson de Roland* is no longer (if indeed it ever
was) a literary text. There would be no objection to this, were it not
for the fact that few works would be spared. Moreover, is a small
group of students and professors enough to guarantee the literariness
of a text? Ellis would probably think not; yet some of the greatest
literary monuments of the past now have a very limited circulation
because of the objective difficulties that have to be faced in reading
them. On the other hand, the divulgation of works in a society is
undoubtedly conditioned largely by a few cultural operators: critics,
historians of literature, the publishing industry, censors, and so on.
The text's vitality, to which Ellis refers, may be distinguished with
difficulty from its "success" (ephemeral or lasting), a factor too de-
pendent on the ups and downs of fortune and history to be a valid
criterion.

Neither do we move any closer to a solution to our problem by
resorting to the historical method par excellence, that is, to the category of literary history, which in many ways is still hegemonic in
several critical traditions. We would expect this discipline to enun-
ciate at least implicit criteria for recognizing literariness. By definition, in fact, the literary historian should deal only with literary
works from an historical viewpoint, regardless of the fluctuations
that the concept of literature has known. But if we take a closer look
at the objects of literary history, we soon realize that it covers an
enormous range, ending up by claiming as its own almost everything
in book form, including oral traditions transcribed or transcribable
in writing. When taken to its extreme and logical consequences,
literary history is therefore concerned not only with poetry and fiction, but also with works of historiography, politics, didactics, reli-
gion, and so on, produced in a given language, according to an
objectively, though not theoretically, limited inventory. Nor would
the suspicion be completely unfounded that all the rejects and cast-

offs (with all due respect) of other disciplines could become literature, preserving at most only a documentary value, once they have
ceased to be topical. In effect, one could hazard the guess that a
large number of the "writers" now appearing in literary histories—
say, for Italian literature, Galileo or Gramsci—would never have
hoped, nor perhaps even appreciated, one day standing shoulder to
shoulder with Petrarch or Metastasio. And we might repeat today
what Jakobson had polemically written long ago: "Up to now, historians of literature seemed rather like a certain type of police who,
in order to arrest someone, would lay hold of anything it might hap-
pen to find in the house, as well as anyone walking down the street.
Thus literary historians made use of everything: biography, psychology, politics, philosophy. Instead of a science of literature, they
created a conglomeration of rudimental disciplines, as though they
had forgotten that each of these categories belonged to a corresponding science: history of philosophy, history of culture, psychology,
etc., and that these latter may naturally also use literary monuments
as defective, second-class documentation" [1921: 11].

The above comments are not intended to profane any sacrosanct
values, were there any more need to do so. Looking at the question
another way, every literary history is an example of how a critic can
see "connotation" and "denotation" wherever and whenever he
pleases. No scandal then if a work that has perhaps contributed to
founding a new science or to the progress of civilization is read and
analyzed as an example of good style, or as a document of the history of thought reconquered by the humanities. Obviously, by saying
this, I am not attempting to discuss the validity of an operation that
views the entirely "literary" text, as well as any other cultural document, as a monument, a moment, or an aspect, however small, of
history tout court, and thus, from a materialistic standpoint, of the
history of class struggles. All distinctions are erased in this perspective, and the literary historian may accept with dignity and humility
the task of discussing and recalling documents that, to the historian,
must be only of secondary, tertiary, or of the least importance. But
at this point neither literary theory nor criticism would have any
right to an autonomous existence, though few as yet have felt free to
admit this. Whatever the case and whatever his viewpoint, in order
to begin his work, the literary historian must be prepared to ignore

completely and to shut his eyes to a problem that usually comes first in every discipline: the delimitation of his field of study. Indeed, any written or writeable text may be included in the hospitable category of literature; and should an inevitable selection take place, the excluded texts will not necessarily be considered as "nonliterary," because both "literary" and "nonliterary" remain undefined. Any omissions (George Washington's love letters, any teenager's diary, Allen Ginsberg's shopping list or even my own) will have had to be left out merely through lack of space.

Note that so far we have mentioned only the contents of literary histories, and not the methods to be employed in their compilation: these latter, too, will be as varied as the former. Thus, recently a critic, in an obviously progressive mood, did in fact recommend that no methodology or branch of knowledge be missing among the ingredients of a history of literature, fortunately still to be written. These would include textual analysis, the history of criticism and ideas, rhetoric, linguistics, psychology, psychoanalysis, sociology—a program which seems ridiculous if only because it assumes an omniscient scholar, but which has already been applied partially and to a more modest extent in some textbooks. In its ideal form then, literary history would become a kind of encyclopedia, in a diachronic rather than an alphabetical order, summarizing all knowledge and methodologies, and at the same time be history in the true sense of the term.

From the above, it is clear that the weakness in any literary history lies not so much in the method or methods used (indeed, there are some works throughout which the same point of view is applied in a fairly consistent and balanced way) as in the lack of any precise delimitation of the field. The trespassing into other, often inappropriate, methods and perspectives is justified precisely by the inclusion in the realm of literature of texts that may not be explained entirely or at all by the most tested critical tools. Because of the presence of these texts, whether clandestine or legitimate, the literary historian faces the necessity of being a philosopher at times, a sociologist at others, and then a psychologist, an anthropologist, and so on. Inevitably, this results in a superficial and unsatisfactory methodology that fails to describe adequately the text in question both with respect to the discipline to which it originally belonged and with respect to the literary disciplines in the narrow sense of the word.

This kind of basic error seems to persist in what is perhaps the most noteworthy attempt at restructuring literary history—"this respectable discipline" that has "fallen more and more into discredit, and not without reason,"—from the standpoint of aesthetic response undertaken by Jauss [1967: 144]. The model he proposes is an original synthesis of the formalistic and sociological methods, and is based on the optimistic conviction that the literary work has a "socially formative function" [200]. According to the final thesis in Jauss's book, the task of literary history "is only complete when literary production is not merely described synchronically and diachronically in the succession of its systems, but also viewed as *special history* in its own peculiar relationship to *general history*. This relationship is not entirely explained by identifying in the literature of all times a typified, idealized, satirical, or utopian picture of social existence. The social function of literature becomes fully manifest only where the reader's literary experience enters into the horizon of expectations of his real life, shapes his understanding of the world, and therefore influences his social behavior" [199]. As a result, "the gap between literature and history, between aesthetic and historic knowledge may be bridged if literary history does not limit itself once again to describing the process of general history as it is reflected in its works, but discovers in the course of 'literary evolution' that truly *socially formative* function that belonged to literature, in competition with other arts and social forces in man's emancipation from his natural, religious, and social ties" [207]. One is reluctant to admit, however, that literature may be considered at the same level as other "social forces," and it is curious that Jauss, too, faces the problem of *Literaturgeschichte als Provokation der Literaturwissenschaft* without first explaining what he means by "literary text." Indeed, one cannot exclude the possibility that a literal application of his proposal might lead to the favoring of works more significant from a "cultural" or "ideological" point of view. Literature would then be handling tasks more rigorously carried out over many centuries by a "scientific" discipline: philosophy, in its branches of ethics and politics. Contrariwise, the whole of philosophical production would fall by rights into the category of literature, asserting itself over poetry and narrative because of a greater degree, perhaps, of literariness.

Obviously, the most tested "sociological" method is that which defines itself as marxist. There is no single type or direction of marxist criticism: we are faced instead with considerably different trends that may lead to considerably different results. What should be emphasized and what concerns us most is how, until now, very little has been done toward building a critique of the very notion of literature, a task to which the marxist theorist should not consider himself unsuited. The debate, almost always internal, on the applications of the sociological method has caused a whole series of problems to be relegated to a secondary level when they are not secondary at all. This has sometimes meant that viewpoints and analytical tools difficult to reconcile with the central theses of Marxism have been accepted eclectically and indiscriminately. The problem of the marxist appropriation of the methodologies and results of bourgeois culture and science again crops up in all its importance. Obviously, it would be both naive and utopistic to liquidate summarily a heritage of experiments and data, even in the field of literary research, that should instead be recuperated and used once one possesses the theoretical premises necessary to distinguish between the instrument and the ideology behind it. In the case in hand, it is superfluous perhaps to stress that a criticism, even though radical, of bourgeois theories on art and literature, starting with those of the giants and ending up with those of the dwarves balanced on their shoulders, cannot and should not reasonably aim at leaving nothing but a wasteland behind it; yet it is necessary to emphasize that only by overturning the bourgeois viewpoint on artistic production and its use can one recuperate and therefore take possession of techniques and methods elaborated in the shadow of the ideology against which all those who accept the marxist hypothesis are sided.

As is well-known, Marx and Engels concerned themselves only sporadically with literature, so that it would be useless to seek precise methodological indications in their works. Yet on a few points they are quite clear. In 1857, in the unpublished introduction to *Zur Kritik der politischen Ökonomie*, Marx wrote, "Without production, no consumption; but also without consumption, no production; since production would then be purposeless. . . . Thus the product, unlike a mere natural object, proves itself to be, *becomes*, a product only through consumption. . . . As soon as consumption emerges from its initial state of natural crudity and immediacy—and, if it remained at that stage, this would be because production itself had been arrested there—it becomes itself mediated as a drive by the object. The need which consumption feels for the object is created by the perception of it. The object of art—like every other product—creates a public which is sensitive to art and enjoys beauty. Production thus not only creates an object for the subject, but also a subject for the object" [1857: 91–92]. These are extremely clear statements, seeming purposely measured to refute any theory (still to be made explicit in Marx's time) of the specificity of literature. On the other hand, the opposition between producers and consumers of art is viewed in terms of division of labor. The very figure of the artist is destined to change and, more precisely, to disappear in a communist society. "The exclusive concentration of artistic talent in particular individuals, and its suppression in the broad mass which is bound up with this," write Marx and Engels in *Die deutsche Ideologie*, "is a consequence of division of labour. . . . In any case, with a communist organization of society, there disappears the subordination of the artist to some definite art, thanks to which he is exclusively a painter, sculptor, etc., the very name of his activity adequately expressing the narrowness of his professional development and his dependence on division of labour. In a communist society there are no painters but at most people who engage in painting among other activities" [Marx and Engels 1845–46: 190].

In the Marxian and marxist conception, therefore, a definition of literature in terms of universals cannot have any place. This means that no definition valid for all ages and cultures is possible, and thus there can be no general aesthetics. On the contrary, just as production may exist only if there is consumption, art implies an audience and is realized as such only in the act of consumption. But we shall come back to these concepts in the last chapter.

5

Rhetoric and Poetics

It is not encouraging to be witness to revolutions and uprisings that, beyond the smoke screen of a new terminology, end up as yet another reproposal of the status quo.

The rediscovery of rhetoric could have been a real turning point for poetics, as well as providing a well-tested means of analysis and classification. But the program carried out thus far by the neo-rhetoricians has instead been very limited: they have updated the inventory, produced many praiseworthy analyses, placed books found in antique stores side by side with paperbacks by Saussure and Chomsky. But nothing has occurred that is comparable to the operation effected by one such as Perelman in the philosophical domain, demonstrating the potentially revolutionary, or at least demystifying, use of the science of rhetoric.

Quite on the the contrary. A first tendency consists in an ever more restrictive definition of the field of rhetoric, to the extent that all interest is polarized on the contrast between metaphor and metonymy, and then exclusively on metaphor. As a consequence, rhetoric has been reduced to the figures of discourse alone, which may all be led back to one or two hegemonic figures.

Èjxenbaum, in a volume on Anna Axmatova [1923], and later

Jakobson, in an essay on Pasternak [1935*b*], had already likened metonymy to prose and metaphor to poetry. In 1956 Jakobson reformulated this opposition more clearly: "The principle of similarity underlies poetry. . . . Prose, on the contrary, is forwarded essentially by contiguity. Thus, for poetry, metaphor, and for prose, metonymy is the line of least resistance and, consequently, the study of poetical tropes is directed chiefly toward metaphor. The actual bipolarity has been artifically replaced in these studies by an amputated, unipolar scheme" [1956: 95–96]. The same viewpoint was repeated by Jakobson at the Bloomington symposium [1960: 375].

This kind of polarization, which in Jakobson could still be a general and almost "metaphorical" way of characterizing poetry on the one hand and prose on the other, seems instead to have been taken literally by the researchers trained in the neo-rhetorical school. And this is not all. Despite the master's warning against replacing the "actual bipolarity" with "an amputated, unipolar scheme," all attention has recently turned toward metaphor. The Groupe μ from Liège, which has provided a new catalog of figures rather pretentiously entitled *Rhétorique générale* [1970], derives its name from the initial of the word that in Greek refers to "the most prestigious of metaboles" [7], and considers metaphor (seen as the result of two synecdoches) "the central figure of any rhetoric" [91], the one to which all other figures are hierarchically subordinated.

The process whereby rhetoric is reduced to *elocutio* alone, to the disadvantage of *inventio*, *dispositio*, *memoria*, and *actio*, did indeed originate much earlier. Over the last few centuries, the study of rhetoric has been drawn progressively into the sphere of literary disciplines, thus being deprived of what was originally its principal aim: to intervene on reality by means of words, and to modify the situation in which the speaker or writer finds himself. According to Genette [1972: 21–40], this trend may be traced back at least as far as the classical French rhetoricians; while Florescu [1960] believes it begins even before, during the Middle Ages, though its roots lie in classical antiquity itself. However far back one might go, it is nevertheless clear that the rebirth of rhetoric in the sixties takes this process up at an already advanced stage and carries it to the point of exasperation.

The "literaturization" of rhetoric (to use Florescu's term) is therefore parallel to its growing uselessness, which is perfectly consistent with the dominant trends in twentieth-century literary theories. Thus neo-rhetoric represents an invaluable integration into neo-formalism, and obviously, neo-formalism uses it tendentiously. It is, in effect, a rhetoric made to measure for the aesthetics of art for art's sake, a discipline of good style that helps describe the literary text as a noncommunicating message.

When we read in the Groupe μ's manual that "the poetic word is disqualified as a communicative act: in effect it does not communicate anything, or rather, it only communicates itself" [19], the reference to Jakobson is clear, though with the terminological variant of calling Jakobson's poetic function rhetorical function [24, 33]. The concept of the nonreferential nature of literary language also reappears, with the comment that rhetorical structures are not something "additional" to the text, but that their presence helps modify the message radically, to the extent that the arbitrary link between the two sides of the linguistic sign is here undermined: "Precisely because it is poetic, poetic language is nonreferential, and it is referential only when it is not poetic." The conclusion is that "art, as we have long known, and as we forget from time to time, is in itself situated beyond the distinction between the true and the false" [19].

With these premises, we can expect few surprises. Though expressing some doubts, the Liège group ends up by accepting the very widespread concept of "deviation with respect to a norm" because of its "operative fruitfulness" [20], and defines literature as a "special use of language" [14]. But at the point of defining normal usage—the "norm"—they claim that "it would not be wise to take as a point of reference that which for convenience's sake is termed 'everyday' or 'familiar' language, or the language of the 'man in the street.' Poetic language should rather be compared to a theoretical model of communication" [17]. The same procedure as that employed by the formalists (discussed in Chapter 1) returns here. In the attempt to isolate the invariants in the literary use of language, one sets out inductively from (literary) texts and compares them, not to other (nonliterary) texts, but to a "theoretical model of communication," the (nonliterary) linguistic system, once called more simply standard language: any differences are "deviations," and as such the object of rhetoric. It would be pointless to underline again how theoretically and methodologically incorrect this procedure is, although it makes ample use of half a century of linguistic research: but, on the other hand, it is the only procedure possible if one wishes to safeguard at all costs the autonomy of the poetic (or rhetorical) function. The authors would probably have obtained the same results and the same catalog of figures if they had compared the *parole* of a man in the street to the linguistic system, thereby exemplifying an often quoted comment of Du Marsais's (which they themselves cite) that "more figures are born on a market day than in several days of academical sessions." Once more, the real existence of what Saussure called *langue* and Hjelmslev a denotative semiotic is taken for granted: these abstract models are now instrumentally hypostatized to give birth, not to new models, but to fading phantoms.

The amount of space that has been given over to the discussion of the *Rhétorique générale* is due to the fact that this is undoubtedly the most ambitious work produced in neo-rhetorical milieux. But a glance at other recent works on rhetoric, if we exclude the more cautious approach of Genette [1966; 1969; 1972], Kibedi Varga [1970], and a few others, would lead us to the same conclusions. Cohen [1966] believes that all figures aim at provoking the metaphorical process, while Albert Henry, though moving from a different standpoint, gives metonymy and metaphor (in a new hierarchical order) a privileged position among tropes, both generated by "a single essential mental operation" [1971: 10]. Le Guern [1973] diligently applies Jakobson's theory of the two figures; Delas and Filliolet [1973] that of the poetic function. Todorov, for his part, criticizes the notion of a mythical "natural" language [1967: 97–105] but also maintains that "poetic language is not only foreign to good usage; it is its antithesis. Its essence consists in violating the norms of language; and if its influence is such that ordinary language accepts the violation as a new norm, poetry assails other rules, other laws, that had so far remained intact" [1965: 305] (though one might mention his more recent palinode [1973–74], which reaches much more skeptical conclusions.)

The doubts I have expressed about these works do not imply a negative judgment on all of them. Normally one uses the tools he finds on the market, for the simple reason that it would be impossible for him to make his own hammer and nails each time he has to hang a picture on the wall. And nobody wants to cast the first stone here. Nevertheless, things begin to get tiresome when the same tools, dusted and polished, have been passing from hand to hand for nearly a century, and there are still people who claim to have invented new ones. Yet it would be shortsighted to ignore the developments and the considerable accumulation of data that has occurred over the last decades. In particular, while it is true that rhetoric has gradually been stripped and deprived of important sectors, the study of figures has grown more refined and has widened its horizon to include syntactic and narrative structures, an indispensable premise for a reexamination of prose in a new light. On the other hand, very little has been achieved on the side of nonliterary rhetoric, in order to take into account at last the figures produced by the man in the street on market day to which the laureate figures of the poets might be juxtaposed. The old distinction between figures of usage and figures of invention, however, must necessarily be reexamined, first, because figures of usage must originally have been figures of invention, and also because this is really a single, indivisible phenomenon—nor can one claim that figures of invention belong to men of letters alone.

From our standpoint, and in a less suffocating conception of the communicative process, the study of rhetoric, before being a part of poetics, should find its place in the linguistic discipline analyzing the connotative semiotics, for tropes of any kind or dimension in themselves express connotators, some of which are solidary with particular systems of semiotic usage, others with particular systems of semiotic schemes. Any rhetorically instrumentated use of language, in fact, expresses connotators provided by the figures of *elocutio*, by those of narration, and by other techniques of rhetoric, whether codified or codifiable. In this sense, the most trivial of metaphors that may have entered everyday speech constitutes a connotator along with the most complex, contrived construction of discourse, organization of parts, and so on, in a scientific, philosophical, political, or narrative text. Thus, one should exclude all possibility of a "transparent" language free from any rhetorical colors: classical rhetoric itself lists and analyzes discourses that seemingly avoid any rhetorical artifice. "Plain" discourse, therefore, does not coincide at all with what Hjelmslev terms a denotative semiotic, but is itself the result of the speaker's or writer's strategic choice, in relation, of course, to his repertoire and his degree of competence of the various uses of language.

If one accepts this point of view, then rhetoric enters into linguistics as the analysis of the connotators solidary with the functives of a denotative semiotic. As we already know, a sign function is set up between the denotative semiotic and the connotators (that is, between the two planes, expression and content, of the connotative semiotic): so, here too, the principle is valid according to which "both the study of expression and the study of content are a study of the relation between expression and content; these two cannot therefore be isolated from each other without serious harm" [Hjelmslev 1943: 75]. This means that rhetoric cannot be kept apart from linguistics: in conjunction with linguistics, it should become a synchronic discipline, descriptive and not normative, no longer limited to literary texts alone.

By modifying the procedures of analysis (from inductive to deductive) and widening its field of action, this rhetoric would necessarily differentiate itself from traditional rhetoric, since it would have to be prepared to describe any possible (or only virtually possible) text, and not merely a relatively restricted number of texts, easily traceable to well-defined cultural traditions. I believe that the task of revising rhetorical categories should be tackled in this light, definitely increasing their number but at the same time freeing the analysis of content-form from purport, because in this case too, "the *content-form* . . . is independent of, and stands in arbitrary relationship to, the *purport*, and forms it into a *content-substance*" [Hjelmslev 1943: 52]. There is no reason, for example, why rhetoric as a descriptive discipline should restrict itself to the three traditional *genera: deliberativum, iudiciale, demonstrativum*. It is certainly true, as Lanham remarks, that "the form of the oration has governed a good deal of writing and speaking not specifically rhetorical. Its structure has influenced the way we think and argue, of course, in every instance we argue a case. . . . The ingredients of the form, then, vary considerably, but the form itself is used, albeit unknowingly, by an enormous number of people" [1969: 112–13]. Nevertheless, the three *genera* of classical rhetoric actually correspond to only three of the situations in which the speaker (an exceptional speaker, the orator) may find himself, while others may be possible. We must turn to an anthropologist, Erving Goffman, for some remarks of considerable importance to the study of rhetoric, and more generally to the analysis of a text's connotative aspects. Goffman observes that the "situation" is a particularly rebellious kind of social correlate of language: "Is the speaker talking to the same or opposite sex, subordinate or superordinate, one listener or many, someone right there or on the phone; is he reading a script or talking spontaneously; is the occasion formal or informal, routine or emergency? Note that it is not the attributes of social structure that are here considered, such as age or sex, but rather the value placed on these attributes as they are acknowledged in the situation current and at hand" [1964: 62]. Obviously, all these situations make up the content-purport with which the connotators establish an arbitrary relationship that may vary from language to language and from culture to culture. What I am trying to say is that the connotators associated with such situations also deserve to be analyzed in rhetorical terms, assigning the study of the various content-purports to a higher level of the analysis, namely, to the metasemiotic of the connotative semiotic.

Finally, in at least one respect this rhetoric would be closer to ancient rhetoric than is the new rhetoric, by showing a more equitable interest in *inventio* and *dispositio*. The classical division of rhetoric into *inventio*, *dispositio*, and *elocutio* must therefore be considered as an organization, into different levels, of the analysis of the connotators intervening in functives of various degrees. Of the two remaining parts besides these—*actio*, or *pronunciatio*, and *memoria* (the latter being added during the Hellenistic period), usually ignored in modern treatises—*actio*, should be reconsidered (and preferably renamed), for it certainly cannot be reduced to a stock of devices and techniques for the orator. We should, in fact, remember that the medium represents a connotator, as do also the tone and the physiognomy in the spoken language. Alongside these connotators must be analyzed the specific connotators of the graphic system— the use of a blank space at the end of each line of poetry and of particular typographical devices, the layout of the text on the page, and so on. At yet another level, the analysis of figures involves semantics, included in metasemiology by Hjelmslev [1943: 120–25]. Specific studies in this field, starting out from different viewpoints, are already under way, dealing mainly with the semantics of metaphor (see, for instance, Bickerton [1969], Eco [1971: 93–125], Matthews [1971], Abraham [1975], van Dijk [1975], Guenthner [1975], Wissman Bruss [1975], Mooij [1976], and Alinei, who foresees a use of his model of semantic analysis for a "rigorous study of metaphor" [1974: 217]).

If one agrees with the perspective outlined here, or at least admits that one may legitimately move in this direction, then it is clear that the range of a rhetoric thus conceived will be much wider than that of neo-rhetoric. On the other hand, to return to the present state of affairs, the neo-rhetorical concept of figure and its development in other areas, and especially within Lacanian psychoanalysis, have led to some new and freer attempts at redefining the literary fact. Thus, while in 1967 Todorov still took care not to identify figural language with poetic language, Orlando's attitude is much more open [1971; 1973].

Orlando, too, begins with Jakobson: "In those instances where we take for granted that the poetic function is dominant . . . we are speaking of a literary work" [1973: 125]. Nevertheless, as his reasoning proceeds, this extremely limited perspective is overcome and a much more comprehensive concept of literature postulated. The literary text is defined on the basis of an ineliminable figurality rate [164]. Poetry easily fits into this definition, but so does the joke. The notion of figure, in fact, does not consist merely in Jakobson's phonic figure, nor in the tropes of traditional rhetoric, but includes every conceivable type of figure: "Figures of the signifier, figures of the signified, figures of meter and of rhyme, figures of grammar, figures of syntax, figures of logic, figures of the relationship to real facts, figures of narrative, figures of the succession of various sections of the text, figures of the addressee and addresser as internal functions of the text, figures of the physical support of the language, figures of departure from already established conventional figures, and so on. In some cases the figure will be contained in the space of a couple of lines of text; in others its space will be the thousands of pages constituting an entire immense work" [166]. A baroque sonnet or a scientific treatise are therefore instances of different forms and degrees of figurality, but it is the very presence of figures, in any form or degree, that qualifies these texts as literary.

In effect, such a broad definition includes everything, or almost, within literature, from Góngora's lyrics to Galileo's scientific works to the joke. "Literature," then, could appear as merely a useless synonym of "linguistic act" ("text," in Hjelmslev's terms), or as a simple, generic designation of objects, disposing of more appropriate names (poetic, narrative, scientific, philosophical, critical writing, and the like). Orlando consistently admits that he is not interested in "the text's destination, which is purely literary or perhaps totally heterogeneous" [168]. Yet the concept of literature does not become totally superfluous, for if a text qualifies as literature on a quantitive basis—that is, on the basis of its figurality rate—then the degree of literariness varies as the figural patrimony varies. Within the Freudian theory put forward by Orlando, "according to an open definition, so to speak, literature is any verbal language of the conscious ego (written or oral) which pays to the unconscious, in large or very large measure, the tribute represented by the figure" [169–70]. All texts could be set out along a scale expressing their degree of literariness in a hierarchical order that has nothing to do with aesthetic evaluations nor with traditional or historically identified conceptions of literature. In this hierarchy, it might be possible for an anonymous joke to gain more points in figurality than *Madame Bovary*, if one could measure forms of figurality that are probably different in terms of absolute values. No scandal here either, since we began by abandoning any perspective implying distinctions made on aesthetic bases, and we should perhaps note how Orlando's position turns out to be more permissive than Jakobson's, even though he moves from him. Nevertheless, Orlando himself introduces a new element that upsets the original hierarchy, based entirely on the figurality rate, thereby establishing a new scale of literariness. His final hypothesis is that in great literature there always exists "an a priori homogeneity, sympathy, and solidarity" between the presence of figures (formal return of the repressed) and an ideologically tendentious discourse (return of the repressed as content-purport); only this latter is able to motivate and justify a figural density that would otherwise be gratuitous and passive. "This is an hypothesis that favors examples of literature in which purport and form unify their return of the repressed, and it contrasts them with the examples in which we may consider either an ideological purport, which does not give rise to a return of the repressed, or a return of the repressed which is purely and superficially formal" [174].

This hypothesis (whether one agrees or not with all the arguments leading to it) at last represents something new in the history of contemporary literary theories, marking a first step toward overcoming the opposition between formalistic methods and those based on sociological and ideological analysis. More important still, the postulate of the nonreferentiality of literary language is implicitly but firmly rejected. The literary work does not limit itself to describing or reflecting contemporary reality but, in the author's view, can in some cases express an eversive attitude toward established order. It is no accident that these proposals, though discussed in detail by Freudian, Lacanian, and Marxian philologists, did not receive the response one would have expected, precisely because of their lack of conformism. In this sense, Orlando's model remains a unique precedent, which one hopes will find a more adequate context in the future.

6

The Use of Literature

The conclusions to be drawn from this inquiry into the notion of literariness seem at first sight anything but reassuring. The major schools of twentieth-century literary theory more or less openly avoid any definition of the object of their study. And curiously, this occurs precisely in the century that has undoubtedly produced the most considerable amount of analysis and theoretical research. One might say that the more advanced and refined the investigation becomes, the more difficult is the recognition of the limits and specificity of the literary fact, a problem, this, that seemed much clearer in other ages.

If a common and "dominant" aspect may be drawn from the various approaches of contemporary critical thought, it is the postulate of the nonreferential nature of literature. The literary work, it is claimed, is a vehicle for messages that are neither true nor false; literary communication—providing one may still speak of communication—eludes the normal criteria of judgement valid for any other kind of utterance. In these terms, all that remains for literature is a decorative, contemplative, or, at most, consolatory function; and even those who reject "the lie of art as disinterested contemplation" are obliged to admit that the eversive potential of great works "does not usually coincide with a power to modify the world in practice," and that this truth "must be vigorously reiterated in order to avoid illusions about the literary art, or the constraints imposed upon it" [Orlando 1973: 174]. Literature, therefore, is a luxury, just as all useless goods belong to the sphere of luxury; and this would explain why literature has normally been, and still is, a monopoly of the ruling class, or of groups moving toward a position of power, even though some stowaways from the repressed classes may be hiding in the writers' ranks.

In spite of Jauss's optimism, very few literary works have had any effect on historic reality and social relationships. It is one thing, however, to take note of a real situation, trying to explain it histori-cally; it is another to consider this condition as absolute, and postu-late nonreferentiality as an intrinsic property of literary language. One may even agree with the formalists of the first and last genera-tion about the prevalently nonreferential character of a large number of contemporary (Western) literary products, but this is obviously too limited a sample—even if one were to ignore all the excep-tions—on which to base a general theory of literature. Yet with the formalists and all the aesthetics of *art pour l'art*, we are in the pres-ence of an instructive distortion, for it underlines the close ties be-tween literary production and reflection upon it. In a society no longer requiring anything, or almost anything, from art, which makes museum pieces even of contemporary or avant-garde works, art is quite ready to look inward, setting itself apart to the point of rejecting communication. Meantime, aesthetics and critical theories make the best of the situation, proclaiming the theorem of the uni-versal uselessness of any artistic object. Despite a number of nu-ances and concessions, this view never questions the assumption that the poetic or aesthetic function exists for its own sake, and that literature and art are above any form of utilitarianism.

It would be most instructive to undertake an exhaustive compari-son between twentieth-century aesthetics and literary theories, and the poetics and manifestos of literary and artistic movements. Such a project has thus far been carried out only partially. The links be-tween the formalist school and Russian futurism, for instance, are well-known; but the investigation should go back much earlier, to the middle of the last century. We find some interesting remarks on this subject by Giorgio Agamben, who believes that the notion of the self-sufficiency of art originated with Baudelaire. After a visit to the Universal Exhibition, held in Paris in 1855, Baudelaire was left with the impression that commodities "had ceased to be innocent objects whose enjoyment and meaning ended in their practical use," thereby anticipating, in a prescientific form, the Marxian concept of commodities as fetishes. "Baudelaire's greatness in the face of the encroachment of commodities lay in the fact that he responded to it by transforming the work of art itself into a commodity and a fetish. That is, in the work of art, too, he separated the use-value from the exchange-value, its traditional authority from its authenticity. From this derives his implacable polemics against any utilitarian interpretation of poetry and the tenacity with which he claimed that poetry has no other end but itself. . . . The aura of cold aloofness that begins to surround the work of art from this point on is the equivalent of the character of fetish that the exchange-value imparts to commodities" [1977: 50–51].

The notion of the autonomy of art must therefore be traced back to a specific historical and cultural context, and it is first polemically proclaimed around the middle of the last century. Later, these programmatic declarations gradually penetrated aesthetic circles (Croce's *Estetica* was first published in 1902). Having avoided the aesthetic perspective, the Russian formalists attempted to identify the mark and essence of literariness in the literary work's very language. Formalism died out in Russia at the end of the twenties; it was, however, to form a school, first of all in Prague, and then to be rediscovered in France and in the Soviet Union itself during the sixties. Moreover, one cannot exclude the polygenesis of the formalist-structuralist method in Europe and America, as Segre [1970: 327–28] suggests. Thus, it is clear why one is essentially justified in extending the term "formalism" to the dominant trends in twentieth-century literary theory, including authors still active in the late seventies and early eighties. The premises from which the earliest formalists moved do not seem to have changed substantially, and, if anything, we are facing a stiffening of the often nuanced positions of early formalism. As we have seen so far, these premises consist in the progressive emptying of literary language of any communicative function, and in considering the literary text as existing for its own sake, with no practical aims or any capacity to influence reality in any way whatsoever. The nineteenth-century canon of *art pour l'art* is given a belated and obstinate theorization in twentieth-century formalisms, with systematic recourse to the tools provided by linguistics and semiotics. Yet that which had originally been conceived as a polemical program of intervention in a particular literary context is endowed, by contemporary scholars of poetics, with the universal validity of scientific truths, to the point of proposing it as the basis of every definition of the literary. By starting out from a series of texts (mainly symbolist and futurist poetry) in which the rejection of communication, or, in any case, of all practical aims, could amount to a voluntary choice, the formalists have built up a theory of the uselessness of art whose range must be strictly confined within a bourgeois conception of artistic and literary phenomena.

Within this panorama there are nevertheless some more cautious, historicizing standpoints that keep different forms of artistic production separate. Prieto, for instance, maintains that one should distinguish between works of art "in which the basic operation is merely a pretext for connotation" and which, therefore, do not allow for a decipherment limited to that basic operation, and works of art for which a decipherment "that is limited to the basic operation already possesses a meaning in itself, even if it does not reach the 'artistic content.'" In the first case, when "the operation at the base of a work of art has thus been 'defunctionalized,' . . . we would be dealing with a work of 'fiction.' This definition fits perfectly the novel or the fictional film, the architectural fiction constituted, for example, by an arch of triumph, or the products of that essentially 'fictional' art that is jewelry. On the other hand, it excludes works that undoubtedly are not fiction, such as the documentary film, the portrait, the religious painting, or, naturally, the house, the bridge, the chair. . . . Once there is artistic fiction, then the decipherment of the work of art at the level of the basic operation, which is within the reach of the majority of members of the social group, is meaningful only if it leads to the connotative decipherment, restricted to a minority." And this would confirm the hypothesis "of a link between the fact that artistic fiction has become the norm in the production of works of art and the advent of the bourgeois order" [1975: 74–75]. I would tend to underwrite this viewpoint but for the fact that it is not always easy, in practice, to distinguish between fiction and nonfiction. Apart from a considerable number of hybrids (epic; historical drama, novels, and films; etc.), the case often occurs in which a single content is proposed and accepted as fictional or nonfictional according to the author's and audience's attitude: one need only think of the different use to which the same mythological heritage is put in the Homeric epic and in the proem of the *De rerum natura*, and many of the comments made about the poetic function could be repeated here. On the other hand, the basic operation of a fictional drama or novel may sometimes have a primary role—for instance, as ideological discourse—without being subordinated to connotative communication. Finally, Prieto is right in underlining the relationship between fictional art and the advent of the bourgeois order, so long as one is not obliged to deny the existence and legitimacy of "fiction," as Prieto understands it, in historical contexts other than the present. Though one may agree that the connotative decipherment of much of modern art is a prerogative of the ruling classes, this is not always true: presumably it is not true for the minor arts of artisan tradition; for popular poetry, song, and dance; and so on. Neither would one wish for the compromise of a mutilated and incomplete art. The feature characterizing the manner of conceiving art within bourgeois society seems rather to be that the defunctionalization of the basic operation, as Prieto puts it, also comes about when this operation is much more than a mere pretext for connotation. In other words, before being defunctionalized by the work's author (which is not the case for all the artistic products since the advent of the bourgeoisie), the basic operation would be neutralized from the outset by the addressee and illicitly dropped at the moment of reception. A similar attitude is quite clear in the manner of dealing with works, past and present, that are not at all inclined to give up the basic operation.

   Thus, the incapacity to modify the world through literature does not so much depend on the noncommunicative quality of the literary discourse in itself as on its provenance, its destination, and its circulation within society. Besides, it is only by admitting that literature is harmless that one may found theories viewing the text as an exaltation of the repressed (whether conscious or unconscious), an hypothesis supported by Orlando, as we already know, which helps to explain why the audience (the usual audience) enjoys the work so much. Racine's *Phèdre*, *Les Fleurs du mal*, Zola, Verga, Pasolini, one must admit, may well mean a voyage into another world, a descent into hell for readers who have faith in the established order and who are perhaps assured by such works of the need to enforce that order, no matter whether this is with or without the authors' consent. But in the majority of cases this remains a family farce, played out far away from prying eyes and ears. Luperini rightly observes that it is not true "that art has no influence at all on man-kind: it has a precise influence, in a conservative sense. With its ability to produce pleasure (a pleasure that does indeed spring from knowledge, but which is nevertheless the particular, specific plea-sure of knowledge of a world that the aesthetic form immediately tends to sublime and to transcend) and to neutralize the horror of what is known through its own form and gratifying tradition, art confirms the bourgeois in the belief in the certainty and the eternity of his ideals. It reassures him that he is contemplating the 'realiza-tion' of his values in a well-enclosed area of immunity which, while exalting these values, transcends them into a world of purity that does not require in practice any immediate and consequent commit-ments. Vice versa, in the work of art, the total condemnation of all bourgeois 'values' loses all its negative force, for the simple reason that it is still instrumental to a value recognized as supreme by the bourgeoisie: art" [1971: 172]. This process ends up by transcending, it should be repeated, the writers' good intentions, if any. Likewise, the recent, potentially "revolutionary" novels by Vincenzo Guer-razzi, a blue-collar worker in a metallurgical factory in Genoa, in-evitably have become objects of literary consumption for a progres-sive, or enlightened, or merely masochistic, bourgeoisie, before ever touching upon the conscience of the members of the author's class; and there can be no doubt that these works do not carry out any project for the cultural autonomy of the proletariat.

The "practical" functions, of propaganda or of other kinds, that literature might fulfill (and that I, unlike Jakobson, do not deny) are therefore limited to the social groups literature actually wishes to reach, through books or other means: those groups which are the least interested in modifying reality. Within these bounds, almost everything is permitted and there are very few taboos.

Nevertheless, one may easily document the case of a literature that addresses the lower classes and serves to spread the dominant ideology, to console, and to encourage order, by depicting earthly and heavenly paradises. To this end, one may go so far as to speak two completely different languages, depending on the addressee. A *clericus* like Berceo, heir and member of a selective culture, has no difficulty in making himself understood, if necessary, by a socially promiscuous audience of pilgrims. In other situations, the text may contain two or more levels of interpretation, from the most elementary, accessible to all, to that which may be decodified only by those possessing the right key: a significant example is that of Bonvesin da la Riva, mentioned by Maria Corti [1976: 104]. Thus, one is led to the well-founded suspicion that the high figurality rate noted by Orlando in the most ideologically tendentious works must be interpreted as a social selection of the audience on a formal basis, a kind of linguistic filter for the uninitiated, who must be kept away from a potentially dangerous message, a message, therefore, not harmless in itself, but aimed at addressees who have no intention of putting it into practice.

The reader who had every reason to believe that this essay would be an aseptic reexamination of a concept that cannot, however, be considered aseptic should pardon the above brief excursus, indispensable in order to remove the widespread confusion between the historical harmlessness of the literary text and its universal nonreferentiality. The former must be justified historically; the latter, theoretically denied.

With this, it begins to be clear why some theoreticians show such embarassment over specific works that are enormously difficult to fit into ever narrowing schemes, or do not fit into them at all. To state, for example, as Wellek and Warren do, that literature, even in the strictest of senses, only includes works of "invention" or "imagination," since "fictionality" is its distinguishing trait [1949: 26], helps explain *Madame Bovary* or perhaps *Ivanhoe*, but it tells us nothing about how to deal with the *De rerum natura*: should it be considered in the same way as the *Summa Theologiae* or *Das Kapital*; and, if not, are all three literary works, or are none of them? There exist forms of literary expression that completely ignore fiction, so how should one behave in these cases? Quite clearly, we are faced with theoretical contradictions that make every little step difficult or almost impossible.

7

Literary Criticism and
Textual Analysis

Yet there is a way out of this impasse: a rather unorthodox one compared to current theories, though an extreme consequence of these, it consists in broadening the concept of literariness until this practically disappears.

By adopting Hjelmslev's point of view, we have seen that every text can be regarded as connotative: every denotative semiotic is therefore expression for a series of connotators. In the introductory chapter, I pointed to a possible way of overcoming the opposition between literary language and standard language by reformulating the question in terms of an opposition between specifically literary connotators and nonliterary connotators. The first advantage to be gained from this solution would be to demolish the ivory tower where literature has often been kept, thus bringing literature back out into the sociality of an articulated though unitary phenomenon. The presence of specific connotators should serve to orient the message and at the same time attract the audience's attention. In any case, the literary text would not be reduced to its connotators alone, since it would have a status identical to that of any other text that may be produced in a given idiom.

At this point, we should pose the problem of isolating the specific connotators of literature, of putting them aside, and describing them, in order to restore them later to the text, which should be reanalyzed as an organic whole. Yet we now realize that not even this more modest program is feasible. The analysis of connotators may help describe a text, any text, but it could never ascertain that text's literariness, for we would search in vain for the specific connotators of literature. A text can be attributed to the category of literary objects only if one resorts to purport, to extralinguistic reality, which means to explanations of a sociological, psychological, and ethnological kind. In practice, I must again repeat, only a sociocultural investigation can tell us whether or not a text is to be considered literary in a given age and by a given audience. Naturally, this is so of all kinds of connotators because every connotator must be referred to a content-purport once the analysis has shifted to the metasemiotic of connotative semiotics. But an important difference is that, strictly speaking, "literary" cannot even be considered a connotator, since the literary "overtones" we might observe in some signs or sets of signs are the result of a combination of connotators which, when taken individually, do not qualify as "literary" but, for example, as "archaic," "learned," "dialectal," "figural," etc., which are connotators common to everyday speech, scientific language, and the like. By extending the analysis to units larger than the lexeme, it should be possible to identify connotators of styles and genres, and therefore it should be easy to oppose summarily "poetry" to "prose," for example. But while poetic texts would almost all fit into the category of literature, we would encounter serious difficulties in distinguishing between various instances of prose. Frye writes: "All verse is literary, and philosophical or historical works written in verse are almost invariably classified as literature. We can exclude them from literature only by some kind of value-judgment, and to introduce value-judgment before we understand what our categories are is only to invite confusion. But although verse seems to be in some central and peculiar way the typical language of literature, all literature is not verse" [*EPP*, s.v. "Verse and prose"]. It is, in fact, at the point of distinguishing literary prose from nonliterary prose that all kinds of problems arise; and the picture is complicated if one thinks, like Frye, of genres and subgenres such as the *poème en prose*, free verse, the rhythmical prose used in oratory, and so on.

Jakobson, for his part, has taught us to see poetic function even in messages with no literary pretensions. Those phenomena that seem exclusive to the poetic text, like rhyme and verse, are nothing more than a way of regulating language's phonetic and rhythmical accidents. Any form of discourse aims at being impressive, at persuading the listener or reader, at the most complete use possible of all the devices (of expression and content) at its disposal. Even everyday speech, journalistic language, a radio sports commentary, and so on do not follow entirely free patterns. Jakobson himself provides us with a few colorful examples: "'Why do you always say *Joan and Margery*, yet never *Margery and Joan*? Do you prefer Joan to her twin sister?' 'Not at all, it just sounds smoother.' In a sequence of two coordinate names, as far as no rank problems interfere, the precedence of the shorter name suits the speaker, unaccountably for him, as a well-ordered shape of the message. A girl used to talk about 'the horrible Harry.' 'Why horrible?' 'Because I hate him.' 'But why not *dreadful, terrible, frightful, disgusting*?' 'I don't know why, but *horrible* fits him better.' Without realizing it, she clung to the poetic device of paronomasia" [1960: 356–357]. Or better still, the poetic device of paronomasia has from time immemorial drawn inspiration from ordinary language, in which such phenomena originate. And one cannot but agree with Frye's observation that spoken language is much closer to poetry than prose. In poetry, euphony and rhythm are more or less regularized until they become rigid, traditional patterns, traveling through the centuries. But how then should one classify rhyming slang, this strange mixture of cockney and a highly figural, almost cryptic language, in which individual terms are replaced by syntagmata, or parts thereof, rhyming with them (*apples and pears*, "stairs"; *sugar and honey*, "money"; *fisherman's daughter*, "water"; *never fear*, "beer"; *titfa* < *tit for* < *tit for tat*, "hat"; *china* < *china plate*, "mate"; etc.). Should it be considered a poetic language or merely a kind of jargon? Without having to resort to such extreme examples, Jespersen once remarked that "ordinary language sometimes makes use of the same instruments as poetry" [1905: 220], that is, rhyme, rhythm, alliteration; and Valesio's work [1968] on the rhetoric of alliteration is an exhaustive proof of these intuitions.

If a connotative analysis can help us grasp some of the particular uses of language, which I shall call styles and genres, it continues to tell us nothing about whether they belong to literature or not, for the simple reason that there is no specifically literary connotator, nor any fixed combination of connotators of various types, that appears as specifically literary.

Thus, it is always the audience which decides whether a text is literary, and prepares to receive it as such and therefore to evaluate it from the viewpoint of aesthetic value. The value judgement, in fact, may take place only once it is assumed, for one reason or another, that a particular product belongs to the sphere of artistic objects. It is quite possible, and indeed quite normal, for the author to help the addressee make this decision by inserting specific signals within or around the text to announce its literariness. In some cases these signals do not even touch the verbal discourse proper, but accompany it on the outside, or precede it. A jongleur, when about to recite, would ask his audience to be silent and pay attention; in works meant for oral performance, a particular kind of rhythmic, artificial diction or a background musical accompaniment aim in the first place at underlining the extraordinary nature of the event, at distinguishing that text from every other text possible in the same context. The modern graphical custom of indicating the end of a line of poetry by a blank space also introduces an element which is clearly redundant when rhyme and a fixed metrical-rhythmical pattern are present. Or again, the author himself, with an evident meta-linguistic intervention, may name his text "tale," "novel," "poem," and so on, not to mention the title, which already provides the reader with enough information about how to receive the text suitably. Nevertheless, as Fish observes, "these signals change periodically, and when they do there is a corresponding change in the mechanism of evaluation"; consequently, all aesthetic theories are "local and conventional rather than universal, reflecting a collective decision as to what will count as literature, a decision that will be in force only so long as a community of readers or believers (it is very much an act of faith) continues to abide by it" [1973–74: 52].

On the other hand, these signals may be lacking, and the work may require a less passive intervention by the addressees, to the extent that the audience may substitute its own intentions when reading for the author's intentions when writing. Franco Brioschi observes that if "a text, produced by another culture or originating in a different universe of discourse," happens to fall within a particular literary convention, it "may (by analogies in its construction, linguistic register, etc.) be assigned to literature without having been conceived for this purpose" [1974: 379]; while the opposite case may easily be admitted, in which works are proposed as literary but are not received as such by the audience for any number of reasons. Thus, a text "*is not literary but becomes so*; . . . this means that the reader's function is fundamental. Before his intervention the *text* is only a *text*; the literary object begins to exist only with him and thanks to his attention" [375]. Literature, therefore, is a convention: as Mary Louise Pratt puts it in her excellent study of literary discourse from the viewpoint of the speech act theory, "literature itself is a speech context. And as with any utterance, the way people produce and understand literary works depends enormously on unspoken, culturally-shared knowledge of the rules, conventions and expectations that are in play when language is used in that context. Just as a definition of explaining, thanking, or persuading must include the unspoken contextual information on which the participants are relying, so must a definition of literature" [1977: 86].

If this is indeed true, as I believe it is, then every product of language may be examined with exactly the same tools, and the linguist's work will differ from the critic's only because of its different viewpoint and different level of analysis. One must therefore be prepared to conceive a theory of connotators in which "literary" may be added and subtracted at will, leaving the analysis intact. Paradoxically, the judgement of literariness cannot and should not be the critic's concern.

The experiment carried out by Culler [1975: 59–65] extending Jakobson and Lévi-Strauss's method of reading Baudelaire's *Les Chats* [1962] to common prose (using a passage by Jakobson himself) is far from being a practical refutation of a bold exegetic procedure: it rather reinforces and confirms it by showing the high degree of refinement reached today by some critical tools, to the extent that they not only account for texts like those by Dante or Baudelaire, but may also help us describe scientific or critical prose, and even so-called "standard" language in its many textual manifestations. Whether the method of analysis is always suited or proportional to the object is another matter. Nevertheless, to put the problem of what is "intentional" and what "accidental" in a text's texture means to formulate the question in the wrong terms. First, we exclude the possibility that a text which we do not label "literary" today may be so labeled in the future; and besides, those, for instance, who recently studied the prose of a well-known Italian critic, Gianfranco Contini, used methods that were not substantially different from those used to describe the language of writers of fiction. Secondly, in every utterance—lapsus linguae, jokes, poetry, and, to a lesser degree and in peripheral aspects, more rationally controlled prose itself—the borderline between awareness and unawareness, between conscious and unconscious, should be kept indistinct. "Conscious" operations (anagrams, numerological patterns, etc.) may remain unnoticed by generations of readers, while "involuntary" or "unconscious" ones, having a precise structure and sometimes actually being indispensable to the work's comprehension, may be picked out immediately. If linguistics, from Saussure's day to the present, is the science of the *langue*, then the scientific study of acts of *parole* must belong to a discipline which we could term textual analysis and which will eventually incorporate literary criticism.

A similar program has already been formulated by text linguistics or, to use another, not quite synonymous name, text theory. The aim of this latter, in the words of one of its exponents, is to "modify the hitherto dominant interest of linguistics, limited exclusively to the investigation of the linguistic system, and then, by moving from linguistic communication in its complexity, to study the premises and conditions for the concrete production and reception of texts in the processes of linguistic communication. This is possible only in a program of interdisciplinary research, taking into account the results of the pertinent neighboring sciences (such as sociology, psychology, the theory of communication, logic, and so on)" [Schmidt 1973a: 233]. Beyond the variety of its interests (for different approaches, see, e.g., Weinrich [1971a; 1971b; 1976], Dressler [1972], Petöfi [1971; 1972; 1973], van Dijk [1972b], Schmidt

[1973*b*], and finally, the essays collected in the reader by Maria-Elisabeth Conte [1977*b*]), text linguistics will inevitably repropose, once the rigidity of its first applications are overcome, a whole series of problems concerning poetics and literary theory in a completely different light. Van Dijk too admits that "what is becoming obvious today . . . is that contemporary linguistics cannot be considered as the only source of inspiration for literary theory, not even as the only source for the formal description of texts. Naturally, for some time now there have no longer been any doubts as to the need for a psychological, sociological, and anthropological description of the production, treatment, and function of literature in processes of communication and in society in general" [1972*a*: 9]. Here, I have preferred the more generic expression (which is not unprecedented, and therefore must be given a new semantic content) of "textual analysis" to that of "text linguistics" or "text theory" because of the necessarily interdisciplinary nature that the research will have to adopt when, in glossematic terms, it also considers content-purports.

The premises for a text theory (and analysis), which is the aim and reflection of linguistic theory, were already present, in my opinion, in Hjelmslev, as we have seen. One may agree with Conte that "Hjelmslev's *text* is not a concept on which it is possible to found a text linguistics," since his is "a *sprogteori*, not a *textteori*. It is not a theory *of* the text, but *through* the text" [1977*a*: 24–25]. Yet it is true that for Hjelmslev "the objects of interest to linguistic theory are texts," and that the theory's aim is to "provide a procedural method by means of which a given text can be comprehended through a self-consistent and exhaustive description" [1943: 16]. In effect, the ultimate aim of the *sprogteori* is textual analysis, though by "text" Hjelmslev means any linguistic manifestation, from the monosyllable to an entire spoken idiom, which represents an unlimited text in continual expansion, thereby not allowing one "to delimit individual texts, nor to make explicit their internal structure, their constitutive textuality" [Conte 1977*a*: 24]. But this was probably never one of the aims of the *Prolegomena*: "The theory will lead to a procedure, but no (practical) 'discovery procedure' will be set forth in the present book, which does not, strictly speaking, even offer the theory in systematic form, but only its prolegomena" [1943:

17]. Clearly, any definition of textuality cannot leave aside implications of a psychological, sociological, or cultural nature, implications that are initially excluded during the theory's construction, to reappear later in the metasemiotic of connotative semiotics. Here too, my purpose is not so much to credit Hjelmslev with having been a precursor, in a more or less explicit manner, of some of the programs of text linguistics (credit that glossematics would have to share, in any case, with Pike's tagmemics [1954–60]), but rather to repropose Hjelmslev's model in textual analysis, a model that seems much more versatile than others, particularly the transformational generative model.

Textual analysis, therefore, must ignore that which the common opinion of any given age considers "literary." For centuries, linguists have striven to prove first that the Romance languages compared to Latin, then that the dialects compared to the national languages, have a "grammar," that is, a linguistic structure and dignity equal to the most (culturally) prestigious idioms. Even today, one still hears people candidly state that their dialect "cannot be written," that it "is not a language," that it "has no grammar," all of which are remarks that may be recorded with interest by the sociolinguist, but that do not prevent a descriptive linguist from studying dialects with the same tools used to study a national language. The same may be said of the objects of textual analysis, among whose aims is that of describing the connotative aspects of any text, whether written or oral, in their relationship with the inevitably present denotative aspects.

Once the notion of literariness as an intrinsic property of the text has been rejected, and its historico-social relativity asserted, a final problem still has to be faced: how and why does a community identify and define a particular set of texts as literary? To answer this question we will have to refer to a theory of genres, however embryonic this may be.

8

The Genres of Discourse

The literary genre is generally defined as a set of rules and restrictions presiding over the production of a text. We know that, besides the division into genres, classical and medieval theories also had a division into styles: *stilus gravis* (exemplified by the *Aeneid*), *stilus mediocris* (the *Georgics*), *stilus humilis* (the *Bucolics*). The concepts of style and genre have been at the center of the theoretical debate over literature for centuries, but one should note that from a normative viewpoint these classifications have fallen apart following the onslaught of romanticism and the twentieth century. Yet if one adopts a descriptive rather than a prescriptive perspective, the concepts of style and genre are helpful schematizations for verifying the various uses, both at the synchronic and diachronic level, of the literary tradition and of the different mechanisms at work in the composition of a text. In this sense, "genres" and "styles" still exist.

Moreover, the concept of style seems close to that of linguistic level, or social variety, elaborated by sociolinguistics, though with the difference that styles cannot be immediately explained by referring to the authors' and audience's social background. Between one style and another, however, there is more or less the same difference as between two levels of English: between "colloquial" and "standard" English, for example, the difference is a matter of "styles," not of "style." Individual style consists in the speaker's or writer's subjective use of the linguistic code in each individual act of *parole*, while the styles are true systems within the system (the English language), which eventually turns out to be an abstraction. The dictionary is a good example of the leveling of styles, at least insofar as the lexicon is concerned, since it mingles in democratic alphabetical order all the verbal material that can be inventoried, whatever its origin. Whether freely or not, every speaker selects from the lexicon that part he actually uses, while he has only a passive competence of another portion, and no competence at all of the rest.

It is to Coseriu [1962: 1–113] that we owe the notion of "norm" as referring to a lesser degree of abstraction than the *langue*. The norm regulates the linguistic system's various uses and is conditioned by a number of factors (social, cultural, professional, etc.); thus one must admit that a complex of different norms operates within a linguistically unitary community. Hjelmslev too had already denied "the (in all reasonable probability false) postulate that the existence of a social norm implies that a national language is also uniform and specific in its internal structure and that, on the other hand, a linguistic physiognomy *qua* physiognomy is a *quantité négligeable* and can be taken indiscriminately without further ado as representative of a national language" [1943: 117]. Intermediate levels therefore exist between the *langue* and the idiolect, producing a synchronic stratification of language.

Literary styles proper, or those historically defined as such, may be viewed as the result of a combination of the styles observable in language, thus representing a schematization of a much more complex reality, where some levels are inevitably left aside. On the other hand, all subdivisions are arbitrary and become meaningful only with respect to the type of analysis (or, elsewhere, to the type of prescriptive model) one wishes to carry out. Hence, "colloquial" style may be analyzed further, or, contrariwise, considered as one with "familiar" style as opposed to "learned" or "scientific" style, and so on. Here too, we are dealing with connotators that may be characterized in either a general or in a very limited way, while a very high number of possible combinations are to be observed in practice. In the following pages, the term "style" will be used to refer to the linguistic levels of a given language, and thus will not be used in a strictly literary sense. Examples of styles are colloquial, popular, scientific, normal or neutral, learned, archaic, and so on. In this way, I am proposing to unite under the heading of style the sociolinguistic concepts of subcode and register, as well as those "badly defined varieties, which we may term modes of usage, that use and combine more than one subcode and register" [Berruto 1974: 73]. A clear distinction between subcode and register may be necessary at an operative level, or when studying typical situations (the subcode of bureaucratic language, the colloquial register, etc.), but it does not account for all cases of interference among the different varieties of the code. The notion of genre, too, like that of style, does not seem limited exclusively to literary texts, and may be easily extended (following Hymes [1972] who talks about "speech genres") to any kind of text. Every utterance (and here we are in the domain of common sense) must be suited to its context in expression and content; every situation, beyond individual fluctuations, requires certain rhetorical choices, a tone, a style, and precise contents. If we call "genre" this relatively stable relationship between expression plane and content plane, we are in the presence of a notion applicable to all types of texts and not only to those a particular age or taste defines as literary. Besides, one need only refer to highly codified types of writing, and also of oral discourse, to realize that a relative stability between expression and content belongs both to texts produced and used as literature within a given community, and to a more or less unlimited series of acts of *parole*. A biology paper probably does not aspire to be qualified as literary, but it definitely follows rules no less limiting than those of a sonnet, from the choice of language (usually English, even if this is not the writer's mother tongue), to the terminology, syntax, and division into parts (summary, premises, methods employed, results, conclusions, authors' signatures in a significant, though not hierarchical or alphabetical order). All those who daily must read school essays or doctoral dissertations know exactly what to expect right from the opening lines: every student knows how to handle (results apart) the various sections of his paper, a genre with a single addressee. The same may be said of the unmistakable structure of the dissertation, whose task it is to lay bare even the most trivial details of the study to the examiners; and these are characteristics common to the worst of dissertations as well as to some critical or philological classics that originated in the university lecture hall. One must therefore deny that only official literary genres are codified rigidly: a president's speech, a police report, a judge's sentence, may all appear aesthetically obscene, but undoubtedly they follow their own rhetorical, lexical, syntactic, and even rhythmical rules, rules that in some cases are inflexible, allowing for very few variations. Rightly enough, Stempel observes that "any act of verbal communication may be reduced to a generic and conventional norm, whose components, at the level of spoken language, are the social index and the index of the situation as behavioral units. . . . Even so-called ordinary language, often considered an unmarked code of linguistic communication, obeys an exclusive norm of limited validity (there can be no doubt that the standard language we attempt to describe is no more than a fiction). It is true that the specificity-index varies from case to case: it is equally true that there is no text, no message, that cannot be classified on the basis of its generic aspects" [1970–71: 565].

It would be a mistake to assume that style governs the expression plane and genre, the content plane: both style and genre, as connotators, refer to both planes of a denotative semiotic. It is rather a difference of a hierarchical nature, for genre represents a class of connotators of which style is one of the members, while the other members are provided, to repropose temporarily Hjelmslev's list [1943: 116], by stylistic form (verse, prose, etc.), by tone, in some instances by medium (some genres are only oral, others only written), and by idiom (some genres are solidary only with certain languages). In this way, the genre may be viewed as a particular combination according to conventionally established relationships of a text's connotative aspects, including the rhetorical. This explains why the same style may be present in different genres; while in the rarer, yet still admissible and documented case of genres with various stylistic levels, this member is barely specified, leaving room for ample fluctuations (see, for example, Lee [1976] on the place of the fabliaux in Old French narrative). The same may be said of the medium, which is free in some genres.

According to Todorov, "one must first of all lay aside a false prob-

lem and cease identifying the genres with the names of genres. Some
definitions still enjoy great popularity ('tragedy,' 'comedy,' 'sonnet,'
'elegy,' etc.). Yet it is clear that if the concept of genre is to have a
part in the theory of literary language, it cannot be defined on the
basis of denominations alone: some genres have never had a name;
others have been confused under a single name despite their different
properties. The study of genres must be based on their structural
aspects, and not on their names" [1972: 193]. But it is also true that
these terminological ambiguities derive from the fact that every text
is articulated into a number of hierarchic levels, to each of which
may be applied the notion of genre. If taken separately, "poetry,"
"lyric," and "canzone" are all genres, though clearly the canzone is
a genre included in the lyric genre, and the lyric is a genre included
in the genre of poetry. It is only in this sense that one may speak,
paradoxically, of literary genres incorporating virtually all known
genres: one example is that of the carnivalesque genre, provided by
Baxtin [1929; 1965]. The degree of specification, or the hierarchical
organization of the code presiding over the text's production, may
vary from age to age and from tradition to tradition; while characteristic elements of various types and of different levels may be
privileged in turn in the conventional names given to historical
genres [Jauss 1970a: 82–83]. We are in the presence of a system of
embedding, in which every term except the most generic is embed-
ded in a more generic term, and every term except the most specific
embeds a more specific term. This kind of organization closely resembles the lexical structure of language and its semantic compart-
ments: a greyhound is a dog, a dog a mammal, a mammal an animal,
an animal an organism, and so on. In fact, it does not appear that
this comparison with lexical structures has simply a metaphorical
value. If semantics is the analysis of the content (of a denotative
semiotic), the same may be said of the elements constituting a genre,
defined above as a class of connotators (or the content of a connotative semiotic). The parallel with semantics is also appropriate, for
here too there is an incongruence in the conventional divisions of
genres within the same zone of purport (cf. Hjelmslev [1943: 54]),
whether one moves among different literary traditions or compares
various stages of the same tradition. A study of this kind would help
clarify the relationships and the different modes of organization of

the historical genres—that is, of those disposing of labels which, however ambiguous they may be, have nevertheless carried out a prescriptive and modeling function on authors and literary trends. Yet the analysis of genres should not be reduced exclusively to this, as Todorov justly remarks, but should also lay the bases for a procedure of classifying texts according to their distinctive features and components, whose different arrangement gives rise to genres that often fit badly into the conventional headings. To this end, the analysis must necessarily aim at a textual typology in which the very distinction between what is literary and what is not, and between various degrees of codification (the "strong" and "weak" genres mentioned by Orlando [1978a: 204]) becomes of secondary importance. One again awaits for text linguistics to provide procedures suited to these aims.

The complexity of the code of the different genres may therefore vary without automatically affecting the degree of literariness. A contemporary novel may be freer in construction and less complex than a sportscast without any reader's feeling he is entitled to deny it the attribute of literary. And indeed, one must admit constant interchanges between genres considered literary and genres considered nonliterary.

A good example is provided by the epistolary genre. The nonliterary letter, a written message sent by courier, obviously preceded the literary epistle, which found its first expressions in verse, until the genre was codified literarily by Horace, who made satire its basis, and then by Ovid, who lent it elegiac tones and also invented the sentimental epistle (and the verse letter still survives today.) Almost contemporaneously, following the posthumous publication of Cicero's correspondence, the literary letter in prose was born, and destined to develop rapidly, finding favor with many Silver Latin writers. Cicero had a few Greek antecedents (especially in the philosophical epistle), and we know that in 44 B.C. he had planned to publish, in a revised and corrected form, a fair number of letters, undoubtedly the most significant (*Att.* 16.5). The man's historical importance and the documentary value of his epistles account for the diffusion of texts that were private in part, and not all of literary relevance. Cicero himself distinguished three types (*genera*) of letters: the message-letter, "cuius causa inventa res ipsa est, ut certiores

faceremus absentes, si quid esset, quod eos scire aut nostra aut ip-
sorum interesset"; the "genus familiare et iocosum"; and the "genus
severum et grave" (*Fam*. 2.4.): of these probably only the latter qualified as a "literary" genre, though still largely *in fieri* and subordinate
to oratory. After Cicero, the literary letter increasingly became an
autonomous, articulated, and structured genre, losing all the characteristics of a postal message aimed at a single addressee. The
Middle Ages carried on this latter tradition. As is well known, Petrarch's letters were "published" (made public) by the author himself; some were commissioned, and in many cases they contain un-
likely or false dates and information, despite the feigned sincerity
and immediacy (a well-known commonplace), belied on paper by a
premeditated and pompous prose. A much more ambiguous and
complex case is that of another renowned medieval correspondence,
that of Abelard and Heloïse, "one of the most venerable incunabula
of the epistolary novel," as De Robertis puts it [1974: 14]. As opposed to Petrarch's letter, the epistolary novel, in the form in which
it asserted itself during the eighteenth century (apart from its many
antecedents), referred to nonliterary models and arose as a "realistic"
expedient (in the same way as memoirs and the diary) to avoid the
artificiality of an external narrator. By now, the time was right to
appreciate as literary texts a writer's private correspondence, his
diaries (Mácha), his notebooks (Leopardi), and so on. The same
criteria were then extended to writers of nonfiction (Marx and Engels, Gramsci) and, sporadically, to nonprofessional writers (the
diary of Anne Frank, the letters from the partisans put to death during the Resistance).

   Apart from journalistic witnesses of a quite different kind, like
Samuel Pepys's diary, the private journal in Mácha's day was not a
literary genre in the strict sense; it became so some ten years later,
without having substantially modified its rules. Letters, diaries,
notebooks, memoirs, reportages, are all examples of genres of nonliterary origin that literary taste at some point in time has included
in the area of literariness, either by imitation or simply by proposing
as literature, through their publication, texts completely devoid of
any literary intentions. In the first case, the simulated nonliterary
nature of the genre is constantly underlined, even when the game is
laid bare and obvious.

The same may be said of such traditional materials as folktales that have been introduced into the sphere of official literature, with greater or lesser deformations, since classical antiquity, by means of an elementary operation: transcription, or rather the transcription of one of the many possible variants.

In fact, I would have no difficulty in making the rather drastic statement that only a written (or transcribed) text may acquire the attribute of literary. Hjelmslev [1943: 104–5] was one of the first to deny the supremacy of speech over writing, which Saussure still maintained [1916: 23–24]. This view, rejected by Jakobson [1962a] and Martinet [1960: 16–17] among others, has recently been taken up by De Mauro [1971: 96–114] and radicalized in Derrida's grammatology [1967]. From whatever perspective the question is put, one is nevertheless forced to admit that phonetic usage and written usage are two different ways of producing signs, each of which may be described according to its own rules. Thus, while it is true that "the entities of linguistic form are of 'algebraic' nature and have no natural designation; they can therefore be designated arbitrarily in many different ways" [Hjelmslev 1943: 105], this should not exclude the legitimacy of examining the incidence of a particular expression-substance in the actual use of the *langue*. At another level, speech and writing are conditioned by socially institutionalized uses of language, and are not always, nor completely, interchangeable. Superimposed on the distinction between spoken and written language, and with some degree of overlapping, is De Mauro's distinction between formal and informal use of language. A shopping list, a memorandum in a notebook, are examples of informal uses in the graphic substance; a political speech, a lecture, represent instead formal uses in the phonetic substance, even though generally, "the material conditions of writing . . . induce the user to produce signs oriented toward a formal use," while "speech is the best ground for informal expressions, difficult or impossible in writing" [1971: 112].

These are important premises for facing the problem of oral poetry in relation to the notion of literariness. According to the synthetic definition of one specialist, "oral poetry is composed *in* oral performance by people who cannot read or write. . . . This definition *excludes* verse composed for oral presentation, as well as verse that is pure improvisation outside traditional patterns" [Lord *EPP*, s.v. "Oral poetry"]. Lord continues by saying that oral poetry is characterized by the "fluidity" of the text, that is to say, by the lack of an original; by the identity of performance and composition; by the formulaic style; and by the particular ritual functions that it carries out. Nonnarrative types (the incantation, the love song, the wedding ritual song, etc.) "are ritual in origin and in ultimate purpose." The same applies to the epic: destined at first to narrate the myth, it was gradually secularized until it assumed the form of the epic poem, and was eventually enriched with "historical," political, and propagandistic implications (see Lord [*EPP*, s.v. "Narrative poetry"; 1960]; Vansina [1961]). Thus, Jakobson was quite right in speaking of a "referential function" in epic.

Oral poetry undoubtedly represents a formal use of language, but we have no evidence to claim that oral cultures possessed or possess a concept like that of "literature." Obviously I am not affirming that in societies not founded on writing, a particular category of texts cannot be distinguished from every other form of linguistic expression; indeed, the difference is usually quite clear, since only some texts are elaborated and transmitted from generation to generation, thus undergoing a quite particular treatment. Rather, I am trying to point out that the modern concept of "literary"—which, despite serious contradictions, potentially incorporates all kinds of texts and is based on specific forms of production and reception—can in no way be transferred to a certain kind of linguistic production that originates in oral cultures and that we treat as literature today. Besides, the very etymology of the word, from *littera*, is instructive, and it should be recalled that the term was originally understood (Quintilian 1.1.4) to be a translation, or rather a calque, of γραμματική "grammar" (γράμμα = *littera*). In the Middle Ages *litteratus* is still one who reads and writes Latin, while the category of *illitterati* includes analphabets as well as exponents and appreciators of vernacular "literatures": "Ine kan decheinen buochstap," proclaimed Wolfram von Eschenbach in his *Parzifal*. In this drastic opposition there is nevertheless an element of truth, in that vernacular works principally addressed an audience which belonged to another culture and which for the most part could not read; besides, the normal form of diffusion of the most ancient vernacular texts (narrative or lyric) was oral. It took a long time for the new literatures to assert themselves as such; and the conquest of the book, to be read privately or in small groups, undoubtedly represents one of the fundamental stages in this slow process. Yet official literature does not always look disdainfully at oral cultures. The very fact that these have been preserved, even though to a minimum extent, must be credited to operations—philological at times, at others, merely instrumental—undertaken by the civilization of the written word. To fix an oral text in the graphic substance (to choose *one* variant, to crystalize it, and possibly to attribute it an authorship) obviously modifies its nature and the rules according to which it functioned. It is only when an oral text is transcribed, or, better still, written, that it becomes a literary object. But "literary" and "oral" remain antithetical terms [Lord 1960: 130–31; Ong 1967: 17–22].

At first sight, every text appears solidary with the class of texts, or genre, to which it belongs; this means that the judgement of literariness is normally made on the basis of a set of texts, and not of each individual text. If we imagine an ideal scale of literariness, variable, of course, in diachrony as well as in different cultural contexts, every text would occupy in its class a position, a degree of literariness, to be expressed in positive or negative values. The zero point, however, or the point of discrimination between literary and nonliterary texts, could be identified only approximately, since it would frequently be given by a segment of a certain extension, a kind of no-man's-land. It is important to note how many and how inconsistent are the factors that may influence the text's position along the scale. Judgements of aesthetic or moral value, or considerations of a philological or historico-documentary nature, interfere with the simple opposition between literary and nonliterary genres, to the extent that some texts are removed from the series to which they should belong and transferred to the opposite one. For example, a particular text *x*, that reveals evident features of the literary object, like rhyme, metrical structure, etc., may qualify as nonliterary because of its "ugliness"—one need only think of a bad pop song, a poor verse advertisement, and the like. Contrariwise, another text *y*, produced as nonliterary, may be placed among literary texts because of its sheer "beauty" (again, Anne Frank's diary; or Gramsci's letters from prison, described by one critic as filled with a "diffuse and spontaneous poeticality"):

(a)

nonliterary texts   literary texts

Every text may occupy virtually any position, with any value, on our scale, possibly forming a group with other texts that actually belong to genres placed in one series but are projected into the other series—all of which may give rise to the situations of overlapping and interchange we have mentioned.

At the diachronic level, the birth of new "official" literary genres consists in the passage of some genres, or of some of their components, from one side of the zero point to the other, independently of the fact that their individual codes may later become either weaker or more rigid. Normally, new genres arise from the splitting or combination of existent literary genres, or from the combination of a literary genre (like the novel) with a nonliterary genre (like the letter or diary). The "incongruent" use of a literary genre—such as the epic in a comic context—gives rise to parody, that is, to the genre(s) of parody [Baxtin 1929; Kristeva 1969; Highet 1962].

In theory, all genres could become literary. Nevertheless in our culture, as we have already seen, a preliminary requirement is that a text be written or writable; and naturally, the fact that everything may be fixed in the graphic substance is of little importance. What does matter is what is actually transcribed—a public speech, an interview, a university lecture, and so on (all formal uses of language). Conversely, there might not be any literary genre at all, for every point on the scale could have negative literariness. In practice, one may speak of literary texts only if these are viewed as opposed to nonliterary texts; both series must be present and contiguous, even though one of the two may occupy a minimum space. The two situations may be represented graphically as follows:

(b)

nonliterary texts   literary texts

(c)

In classicistic poetics, for example, figure *b* is realized: literary procedures are highly formalized, the selection of contents is rigid, and only a few genres are practiced (various genres or subgenres of poetry, prosodically well-constructed art prose); this is also the case with literatures, or some stages thereof, that know only poetic expression. An example of figure *c* is provided by a large number of modern poetics that are relatively open toward genres, or some of their aspects, that were traditionally nonliterary and that have been taken over by literature, possibly through processes of overlapping.

9

The Literary Text as a Message

What, then, remains of the concept of literariness?

In brief, from the standpoint adopted here, connotation no longer appears to be exclusive to "official" literary texts, but belongs to practically every linguistic act. Thus, literary language is connotative, as is so-called standard language in its textual manifestations, and the spoken language itself. To oppose literary language to standard language on this basis is deceiving and leads to mistaken conclusions. It is true that there exist various linguistic levels, or styles, and various genres, and it is by recognizing these that we may distinguish between poetry and prose, bureaucratic prose and creative prose, colloquial style and learned style, and so on. Yet these oppositions do not suffice (even if only by contrast) to qualify literary language in its specificity, but only some of its manifestations, such as the presence or absence of verse, of narrative schemes, and the like, because one would have to demonstrate first that it is impossible for all the real or imaginable instances of nonliterary language to appear in a literary context; and this, especially from our late-twentieth-century perspective, would be a desperate and vain undertaking.

Once the domain of connotation has been broadened to include every aspect of language, two possibilities remain: either to theorize that no linguistic act may have any referential (or utilitarian, or practical) functions; or to extend the referential function (and not only in a subordinate way) to literary language too. The first hypothesis may be easily put aside, because it is clear that, despite everything, people communicate principally by means of language.

To accept the second hypothesis does not mean to aim at founding a literary theory whose task it would be to provide the reader with the means to extract "messages" from the writers. Nobody believes that writers possess special gifts of penetration into reality, so it would be vain to hang breathlessly onto their every word, waiting for elucidations about one's own existence or the state of the world. More simply, I wish to deny emphatically that literature as such has no referential function whatsoever, or that, if it does, this necessarily has a marginal and negligible role. The referential function, therefore, may be minimum or close to zero, or it may be very great, without causing the text to cease being qualified as literary within a particular culture. Thus, it is untrue that literature carries only neutral messages, that are neither true nor false; on the contrary, it is never neutral, and the reader can and should behave accordingly.

Can it be that "literature" (still in quotation marks) does not exist? Is it an entirely superfluous concept? Two assertions may be made fairly safely, both apparently obvious, but both worth insisting upon further.

First, literature, as a linguistic fact, must not be kept apart from all other kinds of manifestations and uses of language known to society. Instead of opposing literary language to so-called standard language, one should do just the opposite, while still fully recognizing the various levels on which a language is articulated. Literary language may be diversion or communication; it may help us escape the world about us, or, contrariwise, involve us in historical, social, biographical reality, just like any other linguistic manifestation—a private conversation, a monologue, a joke, a pamphlet, a political document, a harangue delivered in court. Literature may be both useful and useless at the same time and within the same text; the range of its practical intervention depends on the writer's willingness and the audience's attitude. A poem by Brecht may delight us with its well-balanced succession of syllables and rhymes, with its whole complex of verbal artifices, but at the same time it may well carry a message of which we must take note, either assenting or dissenting, no matter if the message is expressed in verse and not in prose. Whether the assent or dissent should be the critic's concern (meaning that these should interfere with the description and eventual evaluation) or be left up to the personal reactions of the reader will depend on the current theories and attitudes toward literature and art. The fact remains that the literary text cannot be cast into a kind of limbo in which a minimum of formal decorum is able to disinfect all sorts of claims. And even if, in a historical context different from ours, assent and dissent meant a certain amount of "constraint" on writers, this would not seem scandalous, for it would be naïve to believe in the unrestricted freedom of the artist, past or present. The problem is, rather, how and by whom this "constraint" is carried out.

Second, the decision as to whether a text is literary or not is always left up to the audience, present or future.

At this point, there no longer seems to be any need to safeguard the autonomy of the poetic function established by Jakobson. If a text is "literary" only if and when an audience is prepared, educated, and competent enough to recognize it as such, then the poetic function is not intrinsic to the text, but depends entirely, it should be repeated, on the mechanisms of its social functioning.

The symmetry between the scheme of the six essential factors of verbal communication and that of the six functions of language, shown in Chapter 2, appears in fact to be an illusion, because it is clear that, of all the factors, only the message is absolutely central and ineliminable: without it there could be no communication. The message may be "oriented toward," or uttered "in function of," the addresser or the addressee, or the context, the contact, or the code; but a message in function of itself would produce noncommunication. The poetic function in its pure state is either the inexpressible or a nonlinguistic act. The scheme of the six factors at work in the communicative process should be rewritten as follows:

```
                        CONTEXT
                           ↑
ADDRESSER      ←  | MESSAGE |  →      ADDRESSEE
                        ↙        ↘
        CONTACT                      CODE
```

and the number of functions (for those unwilling to give up the theory of linguistic functions) reduced to five, suppressing the poetic function.

It should nevertheless be understood that the criticism of the concept of dominant expressed in Chapter 3 with reference to the poetic function should be extended to all the other functions. In effect, there are no examples, except laboratory-created monsters, of one linguistic function appearing clearly dominant over the others. Any utterance simultaneously absorbs at least two functions, distinguishable by means of abstraction; but to decide which of the two is dominant remains completely arbitrary. For example: the conative function, expressed by the imperative—*close the door! read!*—must necessarily include the referential function: *The door, any piece of writing* (implied) are still third persons, whether animate or inanimate. The phatic function in the *hello* on the telephone cannot be isolated from the conative function and could be replaced by an imperative (*speak! tell me!* and the like). In the emotive function, the addresser is at the same time the addressee. The metalingual function cannot be separated from the referential, since the code is also a third person; and so on.

Moreover, the theory of functions has recently been redimensioned by linguists themselves. According to Berruto, "the current terminology of the functions . . . is somewhat metaphorical, and does not entirely respect the criterion of enucleating only the functions that are presumably intrinsic to language. Thus the list of functions seems to be enlargeable at will. . . . In effect, linguists have hesitated between interpreting 'function' as the specific task carried out by language in human society, and interpreting it as the use to which language may be put, the ends to which it may be made a means" [1974: 29, 31]. For Prieto, too, language is "primarily a tool of communication, and . . . this 'function' alone allows us to account for the structure constituting it"; thus, "the various 'linguistic' functions picked out by Jakobson . . . may either be reduced to communication, . . . or are not functions belonging to the semiotic structure constituted by language, but rather functions that objects intervening in this semiotic structure, namely sounds, take on, insofar as they also intervene in other semiotic structures" [1975: 10–11].

The *Einstellung* (the orientation, focusing, adjustment) of the message is common to any utterance and any linguistic function, and is a problem concerning the rhetoric of communication, that is to say, the setting of the message with all the available, suitable, and pertinent devices: rhythm, euphony, alliteration, grammatical parallelism, choice of words and their construction, and so forth. These devices may vary in quality and quantity but are rarely lacking. Once again, it is the genre of discourse that regulates the use, selection, and combination of the expressive means at the speaker's or writer's disposal.

The conclusions drawn here about the possibility of defining the literary text on the basis of intrinsic qualities or properties are therefore entirely negative. Yet this does not mean that a demolishing criticism should necessarily result in failure. Once the structural homogeneity of the literary discourse has been denied, we are faced with a series of phenomena (the genres and their components) that may be picked out more easily and examined either separately or in relation to all the other similar phenomena present at all levels. For example, the category of history of literature could be settled, on the one hand, as the history of a certain number of well-defined genres; or, on the other, as history of language, or history of culture, or history tout court. These perspectives should not be confused, but neither do they exclude one another, thus taking into account the complexity of a reality that cannot be reduced to one dimension. More important still, the barrier between what is literary and what is not falls, or at least is not a problem that should arise during textual analysis, while the task of identifying this border in each age could be entrusted to the sociologist or the historian of culture.

There is nevertheless one aspect of the literary fact as a social phenomenon still left to examine, one which we might almost call "specific." But more than an absolute specificity, it is, as we shall see, a historical peculiarity of "literary" production that had a beginning and hence may have an end.

10

Linguistic Competence and Literary Competence

For communication to take place, the addresser and his addressees must be competent of the language employed. Linguistic competence, however, does not cover all the possible manifestations of language, but it may vary according to the genres and to the individual components of each genre. Chomsky's linguistic competence is more exactly an average linguistic competence, consisting mainly in the ability to produce and understand syntactically acceptable sentences. But other aspects are left out, and most certainly the majority of connotative aspects. An Eskimo who has carefully studied Italian, French, and English "grammar" would not have too much difficulty in understanding a sentence like *piove a catinelle*, or perhaps even *il pleut comme vache qui pisse*, but he would surely be perplexed when faced with an expression like *it's raining cats and dogs*, which is almost as deviant as the *colorless green ideas* that *sleep furiously*. If every speaker of English understands a storm of cats and dogs to be a metaphor for "heavy rain," if certain figural uses of language are now part of everyday speech, it does not mean that this is true always and everywhere. For example, anyone unaware of the metaphor of *ship* for "life"—which is not at all universal—could seriously misunderstand one of Petrarch's most famous sonnets. The same applies to the meaning of words: a biologist's *sequences* are different from the *sequences* by Notker Balbulus, or from Hitchcock's *sequences*, while for a speaker who knows nothing about the cinema, medieval Latin poetry, or biology, *sequence* means something different still. Obviously, everything depends on the context, but if one is a stranger to certain sectorial languages, even a well-contextualized term can be incomprehensible.

As we have seen, sociolinguistics has added new depth to the structuralist concept of *langue*, which results from the sum of various linguistic strata. Every social group is competent of the linguistic level belonging to it, although it is normal for every speaker to have a certain degree of competence of several levels. Moreover, if there are special languages (the languages of the sciences, of professions, of the bureaucracy) and jargons (schoolboy jargon, prison or military jargon), then there must also be speakers and writers, listeners and readers, competent of them. These styles (if one accepts the terminology proposed above), like the genres to which they belong, usually have professional rather than directly sociological connotations. In historical reality, it is true, profession and social origin are generally related, but, for example, the case never occurs where a scientist knows no other language but scientific language, or a poet speaks only in verse.

There are, then, types of competence concerning particular uses, styles, and linguistic genres but still requiring an "average" linguistic competence. A non-English-speaking scientist writing a biology paper in English needs a minimum "average" competence (syntactical, morphological, etc.) of English, however standardized and obvious his terminology might be.

The same appears to be true of "literary competence," a notion put forward, in the formalist sense of competence of a grammar of deviations, by Bierwisch [1965], and then adopted, sometimes with slightly different meanings, by others [Ihwe 1970; van Dijk 1972*b*; Corti 1976; etc.]. Klein's objection to one particular aspect of literary competence, that is, metrical competence (already implicit in Halle and Keyser [1966], then clearly proposed by Beaver [1968], and finally taken up, among others, by Valesio [1971], Brioschi [1974], and Di Girolamo [1976]), is based mainly on the argument that there is no innate ability to distinguish metrical from unmetrical lines, while linguistic competence is "a long and complex process involving both innate abilities and a lot of practical experience" [1974: 32]. But these reservations do not apply to anyone who uses the term "competence" in the naïve meaning of "capacity to understand and use a language" (or, as we have seen, one of its levels or aspects), without implying or suggesting any beliefs about innateness.

Thus, literary competence too seems a "partial" competence. One cannot be an expert in English meter without knowing any English; neither does there exist a literary competence covering all languages indiscriminately. Likewise, in cases where a language is solidary with particular literary genres (historically attested: some Greek dialects, and, for certain aspects, Provençal, Galician-Portuguese, etc.), the writer must have previous knowledge of the language, even if this competence is derived (reconstructed) exclusively from other literary texts. At first sight it would therefore appear that, in practice, the language of writers does not differ from any other special language or jargon: it has an audience (amateur or professional) as well as producers, both of which are competent. But we must underline that "in practice," which is to say, on the plane of the text's social use. If one may in fact characterize every special language, or jargon, on the basis of a series of additional correspondences compared to the code of language, this same procedure, as I have attempted to prove so far, cannot be applied to literature. Thus, it would be useless to theorize the existence of a subcode (or of a register, or of a jargon) called "literary language," or, in other words, of a "literary style." The very notion of literary competence, useful at an operative level, would splinter into hundreds of single competences, as many as there are institutional literary genres, genres of discourse that may become literature, styles, possible forms of expression (verse, prose, dialogue, etc.), media, and so on. Yet in sociolinguistic reality, the process of literary communication is strangely similar to those processes we have observed at the other levels into which a language is structured.

This is with one exception. The difference—anything but secondary—with respect to every other kind of linguistic manifestation is that in literary communication producers and consumers are different people carrying out roles that are not interchangeable. In the literary text, the essentially dialogical nature of discourse takes place in a partial and curious way. While it is in fact true that the writer inevitably addresses an audience, or more simply an interlocutor, it is equally true that this latter is silent, because he is never able to reply on the same level at which the writer moves. The case (the genre) of the correspondence between poets is only an apparent exception, for the correspondents not only talk to each other, but they also produce texts, or rather a single text with two voices, which in its turn is addressed to an outside audience. The condition of dialogue—theorized by Benveniste as "constitutive of 'person,' for it implies that reciprocally 'I' becomes 'you' in the address of the one who in his turn designates himself as 'I',' and therefore judged to be "the fundamental condition of language" [1966: 224–25]—does not come about in literature, where the internal/external opposition is irreversible. The writer may be, and usually is, a reader of other writers and of himself (and sometimes critic and autocritic); while the reader, qua reader, is not a writer. Literary competence is different from every other form of competence in that it comprises two different capacities, that of producing literary works, and that of understanding them. Only the writer has both, but the second is merely a consequence of his role as reader. Literary competence is realized in the confrontation of two separate roles: writer and audience. It is as though the use of language in a linguistic community were limited exclusively to certain groups, while the majority of the population could only listen to them: the code is the same, but only a few are allowed to use it actively. This situation is almost paradoxical, because one may also admit that the passive competence of some readers (for example, and with some optimism, critics) is greater than that of the writers, though this passive competence, however great it may be, never becomes active.

This brings us to what the specific feature of literary production is. In literature tout court, the literary text is the product of an author who may have a name or be anonymous. The writer is a professional of the written word: anything written by him is collected. Even today, for example, Manzoni's private notes to acquaintances are still edited with loving care and published, when their documentary, not to mention their literary, value is nil: which is closely akin to the famous shopping list. The tendency is definitely not new. "Complete works" very often include absolutely anything written that has survived a particular author. This is a significant attitude, since even that which no one would call literary is collected, with the result that it becomes literature in some way or another, once it has been subjected to a treatment usually reserved for literary texts: critical editions, commentaries, publication, and so on.

Thus the author is a special kind of writer; it is his job to write: to write, to publish, and generally to be paid for this, in gold or with a jug of wine. For centuries now, society has delegated to writers the practice of beauty, the aesthetic use of language, and accepted for itself the part of consumer. This is independent of the writer's social position, which may range from that of the humble jongleur, to that of the aristocratic humanist, or even to that of the wage earner "who only has his own labor-power to sell," as Berardi comments about the writer working in advanced capitalistic societies [1974: 47].

And this is more or less what happens in every other kind of art—architecture, sculpture, painting, the so-called mixed arts (song, dance, theater, cinema), and so on—with the difference that in some arts, especially those not included among the liberal arts in the Middle Ages, the "artisan" tradition has lasted longer and does not seem dead yet. The full-time profession of writer, like that of any other artist, may exist only in cultures founded on the division of labor, including linguistic work, to take up Rossi-Landi's expression [1968; 1977].

The same applies to every form of intellectual work. And one cannot help but recall what Gramsci wrote on this subject in his prison notebooks: "When one distinguishes between intellectuals and non-intellectuals, one is referring, in reality, only to the immediate social function of the professional category of the intellectuals. . . . This means that, although one can speak of intellectuals, one cannot speak of non-intellectuals, because non-intellectuals do not exist. . . . There is no human activity from which every form of intellectual participation can be excluded: *homo faber* cannot be separated from *homo sapiens*. Each man, finally, outside his professional activity, carries on some form of intellectual activity, that is, he is a 'philosopher,' an artist, a man of taste, he participates in a particular conception of the world, has a conscious line of moral conduct, and therefore contributes to sustain a conception of the world or to modify it, that is to bring into being new modes of thought" [1932: 9].

Despite the ideological gap separating them, it might be useful to confront these comments of Gramsci's with some remarks by the nominalist Nelson Goodman, who in a book destined to shake up the field of aesthetic studies, insists on the nonintrinsic nature of the aesthetic, smoothing out some a priori distinctions between the aesthetic and cognitive spheres: "A persistent tradition pictures the aesthetic attitude as passive contemplation of the immediately given, direct apprehension of what is presented, uncontaminated by any conceptualization, isolated from all the echoes of the past and all the threats and promises of the future, exempt from all enterprise. . . . I need hardly recount the philosophical faults and aesthetic absurdities of such a view until someone seriously goes so far as to maintain that the appropriate aesthetic attitude toward a poem amounts to gazing at the printed page without reading it. I have held, on the contrary, that we have to read the painting as well as the poem, and that aesthetic experience is dynamic rather than static. It involves making delicate discriminations and discerning subtle relationships, identifying symbol systems and characters within these systems and what these characters denote and exemplify, interpreting works and reorganizing the world in terms of works and works in terms of the world. . . . The aesthetic 'attitude' is restless, searching, testing— is less attitude than action: creation and re-creation" [1968: 241–42]. Although the aesthetic problem has been intentionally kept aside in this essay, I believe that Goodman's critique might help reconstruct (or at least outline) a network of inevitable connections. And it is interesting to observe how even Goodman rejects the possibility of formulating and rigorously defining beauty: "Classification of a totality as aesthetic or nonaesthetic counts for less than identification of its aesthetic and nonaesthetic aspects. . . . Art and science are not altogether alien" [255]; on the contrary, "conceiving of aesthetic experience as a form of understanding results both in resolving and in devaluing the question of aesthetic value" [262]. A pertinent inference from Goodman's reasoning is that art, undefinable at a theoretical level, is necessarily restored to a historical dimension and may be described only in terms of a cultural phenomenon.

The critique of the ontology of intellectual labor and that of aesthetic ontology start out from quite different disciplinary approaches and viewpoints, but nevertheless constitute, I believe, the fundamental coordinates for a critique of literary ontology and for providing the premises of a materialistic theory of artistic production in general.

In a classless society, and hence one with no professional writers, there would probably be no sense in speaking of literature, because all produceable texts (to return to the schemas of Chapter 8) would be qualified neither as literary nor as nonliterary. This means it would be possible to grasp the aesthetic side of every linguistic act, oral or written, perhaps even having recourse to the value judgement, when at present this is limited to "official" artistic objects alone. Every linguistic manifestation could then be perceived as literary in this latter sense; and literariness would be a third dimension of the sign. This is perhaps an optimistic view, but not at all a utopistic one. In fact, it is the great bourgeois art of the last two centuries, and especially of the twentieth century, that points the way to this further, final development: futurism, abstract art, pop and body art, the new music, the most advanced sectors of contemporary poetry, have conceived and produced aesthetic objects that, when stripped of the intellectualism of the original and provocative gesture, are characterized by the simplicity of their procedures, by their polemical breaking of the most complex codes, by their reproduceability, in many cases, at a do-it-yourself level. These trends should not be judged so much on the basis of their concrete results, nor of their poetics, as on that of the tendencies they more or less clearly reveal, as well as on that of their openness to aspects of reality traditionally excluded from artistic or literary contemplation. Furthermore, contemporary theories on art, and on the literary art in particular, and especially the theoretical expansion of "poetic function" to comprise all kinds of linguistic manifestations—an expansion suggested in spite of inevitable contradictions—seem to reflect precisely this direction, involving the consumer as well as the producer. That is, we may foresee the model of an art (art as play, as lament, as hymn, as document) that would not be the monopoly of an elected or delegated few but a common practice coinciding with everyday expression. How long this process will take, and what form the transition will have, will most surely be decided by historical and social factors, for they alone can alter forms of production, artistic production included.

Note

This book, written in the United States, was first published in Italy in 1978 as *Critica della letterarietà*. Parts thereof had previously appeared in two papers: the Introduction was published with the title "Glossematics and the Theory of Literature" in *Lingua e stile* 11 (1976): 325–34, while a section of Chapter 5 was read at the Eleventh International Congress of the Società di Linguistica Italiana (Pisa, 1976) and published in the proceedings of that meeting, *Retorica e scienze del linguaggio*, ed. F. Albano Leoni and M. R. Pigliasco (Rome: Bulzoni, 1979) pp. 199–207. Finally, here and there I have reused brief passages from "Teorie del testo letterario," which appeared in *Romance Philology* 31 (1977–78): 308–21.

The present English edition has been completely revised during the translation. I wish to express my gratitude to Charmaine Lee, rather more than a mere workmate, for her collaboration in preparing this edition. I would also like to thank the colleagues and friends (too many to mention them all) who agreed to read the manuscript and gave me a number of valuable suggestions, as well as my students at the Johns Hopkins University, among whom this book was born.

Bibliography

The year assumed as exponent of each item is generally the original date of publication; in a few cases, the year of drafting has been provided for works that long remained unpublished, or acronyms, for collected or encyclopedical works. Actual references, however, are to the edition, reprint, or English translation given last. For ease of reference, English translations are listed separately, preceded by a dash, following the citation of the original edition. Where no reference is made to an English translation, I have translated the passages quoted. I also believed it useful to list French or Italian translations of items written in Slavic languages wherever available, though page references within the text are still to the original edition.

ABRAHAM, WERNER
1975   "Zur Linguistik der Metapher." *Poetics*, nos. 14–15: 133–72.
AGAMBEN, GIORGIO
1977   *Stanze. La parola e il fantasma nella cultura occidentale.* Turin: Einaudi.
ALINEI, MARIO
1974   *La struttura del lessico.* Bologna: Il Mulino.
ALTHAUS, HANS-PETER, HELMUT HENNE, and HERBERT ERNST WIEGAND (editors)
1973   *Lexikon der germanistischen Linguistik.* 3 vols. Tübingen: Niemeyer.
BARTHES, ROLAND
1964   "Eléments de sémiologie." *Communications*, no. 4: 91–135.
——   *Elements of Semiology.* Translated by A. Lavers and C. Smith. London: Cape, 1969.

BAXTIN, MIXAIL M.
1929   *Problemy tvorčestva Dostoevskogo.* Leningrad: Priboj. 2nd
            edition: *Problemy poetiki Dostoevskogo.* Moscow: Sovetskij
            Pisatel', 1963.
———   *Problems of Dostoevsky's Poetics.* Translated by R. W. Rot-
            sel. Ann Arbor: Ardis, 1973.
1965   *Tvorčestvo Fransua Rable i narodnaja kul'tura srednevekov'ja
            i Renessansa.* Moscow: Xudožestvennaja literatura.
———   *Rabelais and His World.* Translated by H. Iswolsky. Cam-
            bridge: M.I.T. Press, 1968.
BEAVER, JOSEPH C.
1968   "A Grammar of Prosody." *College English* 29: 310–21. Re-
            printed in Freeman 1970: 427–47.
BENVENISTE, EMILE
1966   *Problèmes de linguistique générale.* Paris: Gallimard.
———   *Problems in General Linguistics.* Translated by M. E. Meek.
            Coral Gables: University of Miami Press, 1971.
BERARDI, FRANCO
1974   *Scrittura e movimento.* Venice and Padua: Marsilio.
BERRUTO, GAETANO
1974   *La sociolinguistica.* Bologna: Zanichelli.
BICKERTON, DEREK
1969   "Prolegomena to a Linguistic Theory of Metaphor." *Founda-
            tions of Language,* no. 5: 34–52.
BIERWISCH, MANFRED
1965   "Poetik und Linguistik." In Kreuzer and Gunzenhäuser 1965:
            49–65.
———   "Poetics and Linguistics." Translated by P. H. Salus. In Free-
            man 1970: 96–115.
BLOOMFIELD, LEONARD
1933   *Language.* New York: Holt, Rinehart & Winston.
BRIOSCHI, FRANCO
1974   "Il lettore e il testo poetico." *Comunità,* no. 173: 365–417.
BÜHLER, KARL
1933   "Die Axiomatik der Sprachwissenschaft." *Kant-Studien* 38:
            19–90.
CARNAP, RUDOLF
1934   *Logische Syntax der Sprache.* Vienna: Springer.
———   *The Logical Syntax of Language.* Translated by A. Smeaton
            von Zeppelin. London: Kegan Paul, Trench, Trubner, 1937.

CHATMAN, SEYMOUR (editor)
1971   *Literary Style: A Symposium*. Oxford and New York: Oxford
            University Press.
CHOMSKY, NOAM
1965   *Aspects of the Theory of Syntax*. Cambridge: M.I.T. Press.
COHEN, JEAN
1966   *Structure du langage poétique*. Paris: Flammarion.
CONTE, MARIA-ELISABETH
1977*a*   Introduction to Conte 1977*b*: 9–50.
CONTE, MARIA-ELISABETH (editor)
1977*b*   *La linguistica testuale*. Milan: Feltrinelli.
CORTI, MARIA
1976   *Principi della comunicazione letteraria*. Milan: Bompiani.
———   *An Introduction to Literary Semiotics*. Translated by M. Bo-
            gat and A. Mandelbaum. Bloomington: Indiana University
            Press, 1978.
CORTI, MARIA, and CESARE SEGRE (editors)
1970   *I metodi attuali della critica in Italia*. Turin: E.R.I.
COSERIU, EUGENIO
1962   *Teoría del lenguaje y lingüística general*. Madrid: Gredos.
CROCE, BENEDETTO
1902   *Estetica come scienza dell' espressione e linguistica generale*.
            Milan: Sandron. 9th edition: Bari: Laterza, 1950.
CULLER, JONATHAN
1975   *Structuralist Poetics: Structuralism, Linguistics, and the
            Study of Literature*. Ithaca: Cornell University Press.
DELAS, DANIEL, and JACQUES FILLIOLET
1973   *Linguistique et poétique*. Paris: Larousse.
DE MAURO, TULLIO
1971   *Senso e significato. Studi di semantica teorica e storica*. Bari:
            Adriatica.
DE ROBERTIS, DOMENICO
1974   *Carte d'identità*. Milan: Il Saggiatore.
DERRIDA, JACQUES
1967   *De la Grammatologie*. Paris: Editions de Minuit.
———   *Of Grammatology*. Translated by G. C. Spivak. Baltimore
            and London: Johns Hopkins University Press, 1976.
DI GIROLAMO, COSTANZO
1976   *Teoria e prassi della versificazione*. Bologna: Il Mulino.
VAN DIJK, TEUN A.
1972*a*   *Beiträge zur generativen Poetik*. Munich: Bayerischer Schul-
            buch-Verlag.

1972*b*   *Some Aspects of Text Grammars: A Study in Theoretical Lin-*
            guistics and Poetics. The Hague: Mouton.
1975   "Formal Semantics of Metaphorical Discourse." *Poetics*, nos.
            14–15: 173–98.
DRESSLER, WOLFGANG
1972   *Einführung in die Textlinguistik.* Tübingen: Niemeyer.
DUCROT, OSWALD, and TZVETAN TODOROV
1972   *Dictionnaire encyclopédique des sciences du language.* Paris:
            Editions du Seuil.
DU MARSAIS, CÉSAR CHESNEAU
1730   *Des Tropes.* Paris: Vve J.-B. Brocas. Reprint edition: Paris:
            Le Nouveau Commerce, 1977.
ECO, UMBERTO
1971   *Le forme del contenuto.* Milan: Bompiani.
1976   *A Theory of Semiotics.* Bloomington: Indiana University
            Press.
ÈJXENBAUM, BORIS
1923   *Anna Axmatova.* Leningrad: Priboj.
1927*a*   "Teorija 'formal'nogo metoda.'" In Èjxenbaum 1927*b*: 116–48.
———   "The Theory of the Formal Method." In Matejka and Pomor-
            ska 1971: 3–37.
1927*b*   *Literatura. Teorija, kritika, polemika.* Leningrad: Priboj.
ELLIS, JOHN M.
1974   *The Theory of Literary Criticism: A Logical Analysis.* Berke-
            ley and Los Angeles: University of California Press.
ENGELS, FRIEDRICH
            See Marx and Engels.
EPP
1965   *Princeton Encyclopedia of Poetry and Poetics.* Edited by A.
            Preminger. Princeton: Princeton University Press.
FILLIOLET, JACQUES
            See Delas and Filliolet.
FISH, STANLEY E.
1973–74   "How Ordinary is Ordinary Language?" *New Literary His-*
            tory 5: 41–54.
FLORESCU, VASILE
1960   *Retorica şi reabilitarea ei în filozofia contemporană.* Bucha-
            rest: Ed. Academiei R.S. România.
FREEMAN, DONALD C. (editor)
1970   *Linguistics and Literary Style.* New York: Holt, Rinehart &
            Winston.

FRYE, NORTHROP
1963   *The Well-Tempered Critic.* Bloomington: Indiana University Press.
EPP   "Verse and prose."
GARVIN, PAUL L. (editor)
1964   *A Prague School Reader on Esthetics, Literary Structure, and Style.* Washington: Georgetown University Press.
GARY-PRIEUR, MARIE-NOËLLE
1971   "La Notion de connotation(s)." *Littérature,* no. 4: 96–107.
GENETTE, GÉRARD
1966   *Figures.* Paris: Editions du Seuil.
1969   *Figures II.* Paris: Editions du Seuil.
1972   *Figures III.* Paris: Editions du Seuil.
GIGLIOLI, PIER PAOLO (editor).
1972   *Language and Social Context.* Harmondsworth: Penguin Books.
GLADWIN, T., and W. C. STURTEVANT (editors)
1962   *Anthropology and Human Behavior.* Washington: Anthropological Society of Washington.
GOFFMAN, ERVING.
1964   "The Neglected Situation." *American Anthropologist* 66, no. 6, pt. 2: 113–36 Reprinted in Giglioli 1972: 61–67.
GOODMAN, NELSON
1968   *Languages of Art: An Approach to a Theory of Symbols.* Indianapolis and New York: Bobbs-Merrill.
GRAMSCI, ANTONIO
(1932)   *Appunti e note sparse per un gruppo di saggi sulla storia degli intellettuali.* In Gramsci *Q* 3: 1511–51.
———   *The Intellectuals.* In *Selections from the Prison Notebooks of Antonio Gramsci,* edited and translated by Q. Hoare and G. N. Smith, pp. 3–23. New York: International Publishers, 1971.
Q   *Quaderni del carcere.* Critical edition of the Istituto Gramsci. Edited by V. Gerratana. 4 vols. Turin: Einaudi, 1975.
GROUPE μ (J. DUBOIS, F. EDELINE, J. M. KLINKENBERG, P. MINGUET, F. PIRE, and H. TRINON)
1970   *Rhétorique générale.* Paris: Larousse.
GUENTHNER, FRANZ
1975   "On the Semantics of Metaphor." *Poetics,* nos. 14–15: 199–220.

GUMPERZ, JOHN J., and DELL HYMES (editors)
1972   *Directions in Sociolinguistics: The Ethnography of Communication.* New York: Holt, Rinehart & Winston.
GUNZENHÄUSER, RUL
          See Kreuzer and Gunzenhäuser.
HALLE, MORRIS
          See Jakobson and Halle.
HALLE, MORRIS, and SAMUEL JAY KEYSER
1966   "Chaucer and the Study of Prosody." *College English* 28: 187–219. Reprinted in Freeman 1970: 366–426.
HALLIDAY, MICHAEL A. K.
1970   "Language Structure and Language Function." In Lyons 1970: 140–65.
1971   "Linguistic Function and Literary Style: An Inquiry into the Language of William Golding's *The Inheritors.*" In Chatman 1971: 330–68.
HAVRÁNEK, BOHUSLAV, and MILOŠ WEINGART (editors)
1932   *Spisovná čeština a jazyková kultura.* Prague: Melantrich.
HENNE, HELMUT
          See Althaus, Henne, and Wiegand.
HENRY, ALBERT
1971   *Métonymie et métaphore.* Paris: Klincksieck.
HIGHET, GILBERT
1962   *The Anatomy of Satire.* Princeton: Princeton University Press.
HJELMSLEV, LOUIS
(1941)   *Sprogteori. Résumé.* [Revised in 1943–45.] Unpublished in Danish.
———   *Résumé of a Theory of Language.* Edited and translated by F. J. Whitfield. Madison, Milwaukee, and London: University of Wisconsin Press, 1975.
1943   *Omkring sprogteoriens grundlaeggelse.* Copenhagen: Ejnar Munsksgaard. 2nd edition: Copenhagen: Akademisk forlag, 1966.
———   *Prolegomena to a Theory of Language.* Translated by F. J. Whitfield. Baltimore: Waverly Press, 1953. Revised English edition: Madison, Milwaukee, and London: University of Wisconsin Press, 1961.
HOPKINS, GERARD MANLEY
1959   *The Journals and Papers.* Edited by H. House. Oxford: Oxford University Press.

HYMES, DELL
1962 "The Ethnography of Speaking." In Gladwin and Sturtevant 1962: 15–53.
1964 "Toward Ethnographies of Communication." *American Anthropologist* 66, no. 6, pt. 2: 12–25. Reprinted in Giglioli 1972: 21–44.
1972 "Models of the Interaction of Language and Social Life." In Gumperz and Hymes 1972: 35–71.
1973–74 "An Ethnographic Perspective." *New Literary History* 5: 187–201.
 See also Gumperz and Hymes.

IHWE, JENS F.
1970 "Kompetenz und Performanz in der Literaturtheorie." In Schmidt 1970: 136–52.

JAKOBSON, ROMAN
1921 *Novejšaja russkaja poèzija. Nabrosok pervyi: Viktor Xlebnikov.* Prague: Politika. (Excerpts in French as *Fragments de "La Nouvelle Poésie russe."* Translated by Tz. Todorov. In Jakobson 1973: 11–24.)
1923 *O češskom stixe.* Berlin: Opojaz. Reprint: Providence: Brown University Press, 1969. (Excerpts in French as *Principes de versification.* Translated by L. Robel. In Jakobson 1973: 40–55.)
1933–34 "Co je poesie?" *Volné směry* 30: 229–39. (In French as "Qu'est-ce que la poésie." Translated by M. Derrida. In Jakobson 1973: 113–26.)
(1935a) "The Dominant." [From an unpublished lecture in Czech.] In Matejka and Pomorska 1971: 82–87.
1935b "Randbemerkungen zur Prosa des Dichters Pasternak." *Slavische Rundschau* 7: 357–74.
1956 "Two Aspects of Language and Two Types of Aphasic Disturbances." In Jakobson and Halle 1956: 53–82.
1960 "Linguistics and Poetics." In Sebeok 1960: 350–77.
1962a "Phonology and Phonetics." In Jakobson 1962b: 464–504.
1962b *Selected Writings,* 1: *Phonological Studies.* The Hague: Mouton.
1973 *Questions de poétique.* Edited by Tz. Todorov. Paris: Editions du Seuil.
 See also Tynjanov and Jakobson.

JAKOBSON, ROMAN, and MORRIS HALLE
1956 *Fundamentals of Language.* The Hague: Mouton.

JAKOBSON, ROMAN, and CLAUDE LÉVI-STRAUSS
1962   *"Les Chats* de Charles Baudelaire." *L'Homme* 2: 5–21.
JAUSS, HANS ROBERT
1967   *Literaturgeschichte als Provokation der Literaturwissen-
           schaft.* Konstanz: Universitäts-Druckerei. Reprinted in Jauss
           1970*b*: 144–207.
1970*a*   "Littérature médiévale et théorie des genres." *Poétique* 1:
           79–101.
1970*b*   *Literaturgeschichte als Provokation.* Frankfurt am Main:
           Suhrkamp.
JESPERSON, OTTO
1905   *Growth and Structure of the English Language.* Leipzig:
           Teubner. 9th edition: Oxford: Basil Blackwell, 1938.
JOHANSEN, SVEND
1949   "La Notion de signe dans la glossématique et dans l'esthétique."
           Travaux du Cercle Linguistique de Copenhague 5: 288–303.
KEYSER, SAMUEL JAY
           See Halle and Keyser.
KIBEDI VARGA, A.
1970   *Rhétorique et littérature. Etudes des structures classiques.*
           Paris: Didier.
KLEIN, WOLFGANG
1974   "Critical Remarks on Generative Metrics." *Poetics*, no. 12:
           29–48.
KREUZER, HELMUT, and RUL GUNZENHÄUSER (editors)
1965   *Mathematik und Dichtung.* Munich: Nymphenburger Ver-
           lagshandlung.
KRISTEVA, JULIA
1969   Σημειωτική. *Recherches pour une sémanalyse.* Paris:
           Editions du Seuil.
LACAN, JACQUES
1966   *Ecrits.* Paris: Editions du Seuil.
———   *Ecrits: A Selection.* Translated by A. Sheridan. New York:
           Norton, 1977.
LANHAM, RICHARD A.
1969   *A Handlist of Rhetorical Terms.* Berkeley and Los Ange-
           les: University of California Press.
LEE, CHARMAINE
1976   "I fabliaux e le convenzioni della parodia." In Limentani
           1976: 3–41.

LE GUERN, MICHEL
1973   Sémantique de la métaphore et de la métonymie. Paris:
         Larousse.
LÉVI-STRAUSS, CLAUDE
1958–59 "La Geste d'Asdiwal." Annuaire de l'Ecole Pratique des
         Hautes Etudes. Section de sciences religieuses, pp. 3–43.
1960   "La Structure et la forme. Réflexions sur un ouvrage de
         Vladimir Propp." Cahiers de l'Institut de sciences écono-
         miques appliquées 99, s. M, no. 7: 3–36.
         See also Jakobson and Lévi-Strauss.
LIMENTANI, ALBERTO (editor)
1976   Prospettive sui fabliaux. Contesto, sistema, relizzazioni.
         Padua: Liviana.
LORD, ALBERT B.
1960   The Singer of Tales. Cambridge: Harvard University
         Press. 2nd edition: New York: Atheneum, 1973.
EPP   "Narrative poetry," "Oral poetry."
LOTMAN, JURIJ M.
1970   Struktura xudožestvennogo teksta. Moscow: Iskusstvo.
——   The Structure of the Artistic Text. Translated by R. Vroon
         and G. Vroon. Ann Arbor: University of Michigan Press,
         1977.
LUPERINI, ROMANO
1971   Marxismo e letteratura. Bari: De Donato.
LYONS, JOHN (editor)
1970   New Horizons in Linguistics. Harmondsworth: Penguin
         Books.
MALINOWSKI, BRONISLAW
1923   "The Problem of Meaning in Primitive Languages." In ap-
         pendix to Ogden and Richards 1923: 293 336.
MARTINET, ANDRÉ
1960   Eléments de linguistique générale. Paris: Colin.
——   Elements of General Linguistics. Translated by E. Palmer.
         Chicago and London: University of Chicago Press.
MARX, KARL
(1857)   "Einleitung" Zur Kritik der politischen Ökonomie. In
         Marx and Engels W 13: 615–42.
——   "Introduction" to Foundations of the Critique of Political
         Economy. In Grundrisse. Foundations of the Critique of
         Political Economy, translated by M. Nicolaus, pp. 81–111.
         New York: Vintage Books, 1973.

MARX, KARL, and FRIEDRICH ENGELS
(1845–46) *Die deutsche Ideologie*. In Marx and Engels *W* 3: 11–530.
——   *The German Ideology*. [Excerpts.] In *Selected Writings*,
                 translated by D. McLellan, pp. 159–91. Oxford: Oxford
                 University Press, 1977.
W   *Werke*. 41 vols. Berlin: Dietz, 1961–70.
MATEJKA, LADISLAV, and KRYSTYNA POMORSKA (editors)
1971   *Readings in Russian Poetics*. Cambridge: M.I.T. Press.
MATTHEWS, R. J.
1971   "Concerning a 'Linguistic Theory' of Metaphor." *Foun-
                 dations of Language* 7: 413–25.
MEDVEDEV, P. N.
1928   *Formal' nyi metod v literaturovedenii*. Leningrad: Priboj.
MOOIJ, J.J.A.
1976   *A Study of Metaphor*. Amsterdam: North-Holland.
MUKAŘOVSKÝ, JAN
1932   "Jazyk spisovný a jazyk básnický." In Havránek and
                 Weingart 1932: 123–56.
——   "Standard Language and Poetic Language." In Garvin
                 1964: 17–30.
1966   *Studie z estetiky*. Prague: Odeon. (In Italian as *Il signifi-
                 cato dell'estetica*. Translated by S. Corduas. Turin: Ei-
                 naudi, 1973.)
OGDEN, C. K., and I. A. RICHARDS
1923   *The Meaning of Meaning: A Study of the Influence of Lan-
                 guage upon Thought and of the Science of Symbolism*.
                 London: Kegan Paul, Trench, Trubner. 9th edition: 1953.
OLBRECHTS-TYTECA, LUCIE
                 See Perelman and Olbrechts-Tyteca.
ONG, WALTER J.
1967   *The Presence of the Word*. New Haven: Yale University
                 Press.
ORLANDO, FRANCESCO
1971   *Lettura freudiana della "Phèdre."* Turin: Einaudi.
——   Part I of Orlando 1978*b*: 1–120.
1973   *Per una teoria freudiana della letteratura*. Turin: Einaudi.
——   Part II of Orlando 1978*b*: 121–88.
1978*a*   "Definition of Literature and Literature as an Institution."
                 In appendix to Orlando 1978*b*: 204–6.
1978*b*   *Toward a Freudian Theory of Literature: With an Analysis
                 of Racine's "Phèdre."* Translated by C. Lee. Baltimore
                 and London: Johns Hopkins University Press.

PERELMAN, CHAIM
1970   *Le Champ de l'argumentation.* Brussels: Presses Universitaires de Bruxelles.
PERELMAN, CHAIM, and LUCIE OLBRECHTS-TYTECA
1958   *Traité de l'argumentation. La Nouvelle Rhétorique.* Paris: Presses Universitaires de France.
———   *The New Rhetoric: A Treatise on Argumentation.* Translated by J. Wilkinson and P. Weaver. Notre Dame: University of Notre Dame Press, 1971.
PETÖFI, JÁNOS S.
1971   *Transformationgrammatiken und eine ko-textuelle Texttheorie.* Frankfurt am Main: Athenäum.
1972   "On the Syntactico-Semantic Organization of Text Structures." *Poetics,* no. 3: 56–99.
1973   "Text Grammars, Text Theory and the Theory of Literature." *Poetics,* no. 7: 36–76.
PIKE, KENNETH L.
1954–60 *Language in Relation to a Unified Theory of the Structure of Human Behavior.* 3 vols. Glendale: Summer Institute of Linguistics. 2nd edition: The Hague: Mouton, 1967.
POMORSKA, KRYSTYNA
        See Matejka and Pomorska.
PRATT, MARY LOUISE
1977   *Toward a Speech Act Theory of Literary Discourse.* Bloomington and London: Indiana University Press.
PRIETO, LUIS J.
1975   *Pertinence et pratique. Essai de sémiologie.* Paris: Editions de Minuit.
PROPP, VLADIMIR JA.
1928   *Morfologija skazki.* Leningrad: Academia.
———   *Morphology of the Folktale.* Translated by L. Scott. Austin: University of Texas Press, 1968.
RICHARDS, I. A.
        See Ogden and Richards.
ROSIELLO, LUIGI
1965   *Struttura, uso e funzioni della lingua.* Florence: Vallecchi.
ROSSI-LANDI, FERRUCCIO
1968   *Il linguaggio come lavoro e come mercato.* Milan: Bompiani.
1977   *Linguistics and Economics.* The Hague: Mouton.

SAPORTA, SOL
1960   "The Application of Linguistics to the Study of Poetic
          Language." In Sebeok 1960: 82–93.
SAUSSURE, FERDINAND DE
1916   *Cours de linguistique générale*. Edited by C. Bally and A.
          Sechehaye. Paris: Payot. 3rd edition: 1931.
———   *Course in General Linguistics*. Translated by W. Baskin.
          London: Collins, 1974.
SCHMIDT, SIEGFRIED J.
1973*a*   "Texttheorie/Pragmalinguistik." In Althaus, Henne, and
          Wiegand 1973: 2, 233–44.
1973*b*   *Texttheorie. Probleme einer Linguistik der sprachlichen
          Kommunikation*. Munich: Fink.
SCHMIDT, SIEGFRIED J. (editor)
1970   *Text. Bedeutung. Ästhetik*. Munich: Bayerischer Schul-
          buch-Verlag.
SEBEOK, THOMAS A. (editor)
1960   *Style in Language*. Cambridge: M.I.T. Press.
SEGRE, CESARE
1969   *I segni e la critica*. Turin: Einaudi.
———   *Semiotics and Literary Criticism*. Translated by J. Med-
          demmen. The Hague: Mouton, 1973.
1970   "La critica strutturalistica." In Corti and Segre 1970:
          323–41.
          See also Corti and Segre.
SIERTSEMA, BERTHA
1955   *A Study in Glossematics: Critical Survey of Its Fundamen-
          tal Concepts*. The Hague: Mouton. 2nd edition: 1965.
ŠKLOVSKIJ, VIKTOR
1929   *O teorij prozy*. Moscow: Federacija. (In French as *Sur la
          Théorie de la prose*. Translated by G. Verret. Lausanne:
          Editions l'Age d'Homme, 1973.)
STEMPEL, WOLF-DIETER
1970–71   "Pour une description des genres littéraires." In *Actele
          celui de-al XII-lea Congres Internaţional de Lingvistică şi
          Filologie Romanică (Bucureşti, 1968)*, 2 vols., edited by
          A. Rosetti, 2: 565–70. Bucharest: Editura Republicii So-
          cialiste România.
STENDER-PETERSEN, ADOLF
1949   "Esquisse d'une théorie structurale de la littérature." *Tra-
          vaux du Cercle Linguistique de Copenhague* 5: 277–87.

STURTEVANT, W. C.
See Gladwin and Sturtevant.

TITUNIK, I. R.
1973   "The Formal Method and the Sociological Method (M. M.
        Baxtin, P. N. Medvedev, V. N. Vološinov) in Russian
        Theory and Study of Literature." In appendix to the En-
        glish translation of Vološinov 1929: 175–200.

TODOROV, TZVETAN
1965   "Les Poètes devant le bon usage." *Revue d'Esthétique* 18:
        300–305.
1967   *Littérature et signification*. Paris: Larousse.
1972   "Genres litteraires." In Ducrot and Todorov 1972: 193–201.
1973–74 "The Notion of Literature." *New Literary History* 5: 5–16.
        See also Ducrot and Todorov.

TOMAŠEVSKIJ, BORIS
1928   *Teorija literatury. Poètika*. Moscow and Leningrad: Gos.
        izdat. xud. lit. (In Italian as *Teoria della letteratura*.
        Translated by M. Di Salvo. Milan: Feltrinelli, 1978.)

TRUBECKOJ, NIKOLAJ S.
1923–24 Review of Jakobson 1923. *Slavia* 2: 452–60.

TYNJANOV, JURIJ
1929a   "O literaturnoj èvoljucii." In Tynjanov 1929b: 30–47.
——   "On Literary Evolution." In Matejka and Pomorska 1971:
        3–37.
1929b   *Arxaisti i novatory*. Leningrad: Priboj.

TYNJANOV, JURIJ, and ROMAN JAKOBSON
1928   "Problemy izučenija literatury i jazyka." *Novyi Lef*, no.
        12: 35–37.
——   "Problems in the Study of Literature and Language." In
        Matejka and Pomorska 1971: 79–81.

VALESIO, PAOLO
1968   *Strutture dell'allitterazione. Grammatica, retorica e folk-
        lore verbale*. Bologna: Zanichelli.
1971   "On Poetics and Metrical Style." *Poetics* no. 2: 36–70.

VANSINA, JAN
1961   *De la Tradition orale. Essai de méthode historique*. Ter-
        vuren: Annales du Musée Royale de l'Afrique Centrale,
        36.
——   *Oral Tradition: A Study in Historical Methodology*. Trans-
        lated by H. M. Wright. London: Routledge and Kegan
        Paul, 1965. 2nd edition: Harmondsworth: Penguin Books.
        1973.

VOLOŠINOV, VALENTIN N.
1929   *Marksizm i filosofija jazyka.* Leningrad: Priboj. 2nd edi-
           tion: 1930.
——   *Marxism and the Philosophy of Language.* Translated by
           L. Matejka and I. R. Titunik. New York and London:
           Seminar Press, 1973.
WARREN, AUSTIN
           See Wellek and Warren.
WEINGART, MILOŠ
           See Havránek and Weingart.
WEINRICH, HARALD
1971a   *Tempus. Besprochene und erzälhte Welt.* Stuttgart: Kohl-
           hammer.
1971b   "The Textual Function of the French Article." In Chatman
           1971: 221–40.
1976   *Sprache in Texten.* Stuttgart: Klett.
WELLEK, RENÉ, and AUSTIN WARREN
1949   *Theory of Literature.* New York: Harcourt, Brace &
           World. 3rd edition: 1963.
WEIGAND, HERBERT ERNST
           See Althaus, Henne, and Wiegand.
WISSMANN BRUSS, ELIZABETH
1975   "Formal Semantics and Poetic Meaning." *Poetics,* nos.
           14–15: 339–63.
ZUMTHOR, PAUL
1963   *Langue et techniques poétiques à l'époque romane
           (XIᵉ–XIIIᵉ siècles).* Paris: Klincksieck.
1975   "Birth of a Language and Birth of a Literature." *Mosaic*
           8/4: 195–206.

Index

111

JACKET DESIGNED BY ED FRANK
COMPOSED BY GRAPHIC COMPOSITION, INC., ATHENS, GEORGIA
MANUFACTURED BY INTER-COLLEGIATE PRESS, INC.
SHAWNEE MISSION, KANSAS
TEXT AND DISPLAY LINES ARE SET IN TIMES ROMAN

Library of Congress Cataloging in Publication Data

Di Girolamo, Costanzo.
A critical theory of literature.
Translation of: Critica della letterarietà.
Bibliography: pp. 97–110
Includes index.
1. Literature. I. Title.
PN45.D4913   801   80-52289
ISBN 0-299-08120-6   AACR2